Your Successful Sales Career

your successful sales career

BRIAN AZAR
THE SALES DOCTOR®

WITH LEN FOLEY

AMACOM AMERICAN MANAGEMENT ASSOCIATION

NEW YORK ✗ ATLANTA ✗ BRUSSELS ✗ CHICAGO ✗ MEXICO CITY
SAN FRANCISCO ✗ SHANGHAI ✗ TOKYO ✗ TORONTO ✗ WASHINGTON, D.C.

Special discounts on bulk quantities of AMACOM books are available to corporations, professional associations, and other organizations. For details, contact Special Sales Department, AMACOM, a division of American Management Association, 1601 Broadway, New York, NY 10019.
Tel.: 212-903-8316. Fax: 212-903-8083.
Web site: www. amacombooks.org

This publication is designed to provide accurate and authoritative information in regard to the subject matter covered. It is sold with the understanding that the publisher is not engaged in rendering legal, accounting, or other professional service. If legal advice or other expert assistance is required, the services of a competent professional person should be sought.

Library of Congress Cataloging-in-Publication Data

Azar, Brian.
  Your successful sales career / Brian Azar, with Len Foley.— 1st ed.
    p. cm.
  Includes index.
  ISBN 0-8144-0825-7
    1. Selling. 2. Customer relations. I. Foley, Len. II. Title.

HF5438.25.A95 2004
658.85—dc22

2004010292

Printing number
10 9 8 7 6 5 4 3 2 1

I would like to dedicate this book to the following players in my personal life:

My best friend, (who happens to be my wife), Maggie, and her sister, Zosia, for their unconditional trust, loyalty, and support for my work and chosen lifestyle.

My personal life coaches and trainers (who happen to be my daughters), Emilia and Briana Azar, who taught me more about life, unconditional love, and mutually beneficial relationships than all the teachers, sales trainers, and bosses I've had in my life.

And finally, to the tens of thousands of executives, entrepreneurs, business owners, and, especially, the salespeople and managers who allowed me to enter their space and make a difference in both their personal and professional lives.

Thank you from the deepest part of me!

Contents

Foreword

Bill Gallagher, Ph.D., best-selling coauthor of *Guerrilla Selling: Unconventional Weapons & Tactics for Increasing Your Sales* and *The Psychology of Guerrilla Marketing*.

AFTER HAVING TRAINED 500,000 business and sales professionals over the past twenty years, I get a lot of requests for sales-book testimonials. But nothing pleased me more than reading Brian Azar and Len Foley's new book *Your Successful Sales Career*. In fact, everyone—even the most *seasoned* sales professional looking to attract more business with less frustration and hassle—needs to take a serious look at the principles taught in this book. Each chapter is packed with simple, easy-to-follow guidelines for conducting a pressure-free "interview" that can enable even the world's most *sales-phobic* individual to effortlessly and consistently win over the hearts and minds of his or her prospects.

And if that's not enough—the simple quiz in Chapter 7 is worth a *hundred times* your investment in this material!

I first contacted Brian Azar, the "Sales Doctor," in 1990, for his input, insight, and recommendations regarding the content for the manuscript of *Guerrilla Selling*. Brian's ideas, articles, and programs took a very different approach to selling and the professional sales-person. He was like a breath of fresh air amid the crowded market of sales techniques and sales gurus who were constantly pitching their gimmicks, techniques, tricks, and "ten fast ways to close a sale!"

Brian's approach was contrary to the *"push, push . . . sell, sell . . . get them to say 'yes' five times"* style of selling. He was one of the first "sales coaches" who believed in, and practiced, the Socratic method of "interviewing by asking questions" approach to selling—much like a trusted family doctor, who first does an intake interview including a medical history review. Brian's "Sales Doctor®" approach to the sales cycle, by using an "interview" style, was effective, effi-cient, persuasive, and elegant, to say the least. His ongoing use of neurolinguistics and questioning skills helped establish rapport by creating a "safe" space for the prospect to feel comfortable and do most of the talking!

Brian's friendship, counsel, and information on sales and selling helped me fill in the gaps and holes to order to make *Guerrilla Selling* a best seller. He made a great sounding board by being a good lis-tener, offering positive feedback and suggestions. Over the years, Brian was always accessible and willing to offer his expertise in the areas of rapport building, selling, prospecting, and entrepreneurial and management skills.

What you learn and practice consistently from his mentorship, coaching, and training, will not only bring you success in your busi-ness, practice, or career, but will help you achieve your success with less stress, struggle, and effort; you will definitely have more fun and learn a healthier approach to your profession as well as life and liv-ing itself. As Brian often says: "Selling is only hysterical activity on the way to the grave . . . so have fun. If you're not, then you're work-ing too hard doing the wrong things . . . working for the wrong com-pany or boss . . . or you need a coach!"

Preface

✗ There have been repeated reports that prospects under the influence of this material tend to close themselves.

✗ The Sales Doctor's prescription should not be taken while operating heavily overused sales machinery.

✗ Use of this material may alter your ideas about selling forever.[1] *Do not read this unless you are committed to creating a positive, successful sales career.*

> *You can get anything you want once you realize that anytime you're nose-to-nose . . . eyeball-to-eyeball . . . kneecap-to-kneecap . . . with another human being . . .* you're always selling!
>
> –Brian Azar, The Sales Doctor®

ACKNOWLEDGMENTS

Over the past twenty-five years, I have had the privilege of working with some incredible companies, groups, associations, and individuals, who were open to changing themselves and their environment, and adapting to better ways of making a difference in the world of buying, selling, and doing business honestly and ethically. I could not do this alone. It takes mentors, coaches, dream teams, collaborators, alliances, and partnerships to make something special last a lifetime! In particular, I am profoundly thankful to the following teams:

My writing teams, including the following people:

Len Foley, for his time, energy, talent, and enthusiasm in cowriting this book with such short notice.

Allan Boress, my protégé client, friend, colleague, and MasterMind partner.

[1] The author of this book apologizes for any inconvenience and regretfully assumes full responsibility for these or similar occurrences.

Bonnie Wallsh, the best meeting planner in the world, who has helped keep me busy in the South.

Olalah Simpson-Njenga, for getting this project started.

Grace Cantwell, Carol Foreman, and Barbara Azar, for their unique, wonderful abilities and personalities, who added their rich diversity of style and substance to the content of my written works.

David Horowitz and Gary Thomlinson, for their honesty and special auditory communication styles, which helped balance my kinesthetic preference.

Terry Petrovik, for his excellent visual communication style and marketing savvy.

Peter Tom, for his support and wise council and, sometimes analytical feedback on my presentations and workshops.

Andy Tanen and Kitty Bradley, for their kinesthetic style, friendship, and support for my work over the years.

Joe Arlotta and Ed Garvin, for their special comedic and humorous approach to sales.

Marty Crouch, at www.webvalence.com, and Keith, at www.Triangle webnet.com, for their technical support and Web site talents.

Dan Duckworth, of Voiceovers Unlimited, for his vocal talents, positive energy, and support as a client and friend over the years.

Bob Greene, my accountant and friend, who has kept me solvent through thick and thin, over the years.

Genevia and Ed Fulbright, at www.moneyful.com, for their friendship, alliance, and collaboration on a number of projects.

Ellen Kadin, from AMACOM Publishers, for her wisdom and taste in choosing to publish this book.

Last, but not least, I wish to acknowledge all those companies, associations, bosses, and individuals, who were mean, nasty, negative, and belligerent, for the opportunity to learn the lessons of what doesn't work, and whom I would never want to work with, for any amount of money!

Your Successful Sales Career

introduction

EVERYTHING WORTHWHILE has a price, sometimes in time, sometimes in money . . . but mostly in effort.

That's why it's so important to have a qualified coach, with a proven, undisputed track record of continuing success, who can help direct your effort into the most appropriate areas. And where are the most appropriate areas? Surprisingly, they're not in the place most salespeople think they are.

Look at it this way: Brains and good looks get you only so far. The most successful people in any industry are seldom the smartest or best looking. They're the people who can sell.

How much "smarter" is Steve Jobs, the cofounder of Apple Computers, than his nearest competitors? He's smart, sure; but how much smarter? There are a lot of "smart" people in the computer industry, many who are probably smarter than Steve Jobs. But there is no one (and I mean no one!) who's better at selling. In fact, Steve Jobs is so smart that he learned the fundamentals of sales before he learned anything else.

What If You Don't Know the First Thing About "Traditional Selling"?

The less you know about "traditional" sales tactics, the better you'll do. You won't have any bad habits to unlearn! The worst sales students are those who think they already know how to sell. The best students are those who haven't got a clue. Remember: There are plenty of rich people who would give their left arm to be able to deeply connect with their families, friends, and business associates . . . There are plenty of smart people who would pay any amount of money to be able to communicate their ideas clearly to other people . . . There are plenty of sophisticated people who would love to make more money.

Using the strategies in this book, you get this—and a whole lot more.

There is no other profession more misunderstood and maligned than that of professional selling. Can you imagine a mother saying to her child, "Bobby, you'll make Mom proud someday when you become . . . a salesman!"? It almost sounds like a joke. No mother wants her child to become a salesperson. But here's a little secret: Nothing happens between you and your customers . . . between you and your business associates . . . your friends or loved ones . . . *until a sale is made.*

Of course, most sales trainers won't tell you anything like that. They'll try to confuse you and say that selling only happens at your job. But that's like saying that eating only happens at a restaurant.

The world's most accomplished sales pros are selling all the time. They're selling at work . . . at home . . . at the beach . . . and anywhere else they interact with other human beings. But they're not selling in the "traditional" way; they're not using outdated, silly sales methods that are simply laughable by today's professional standards. In fact, after spending thousands of hours studying some of the richest, most successful salespeople alive (people like Steve Jobs; Larry Ellison, the founder of Oracle; and Mary Kay Ash, the founder of Mary Kay Cosmetics), I came upon two very surprising realizations:

1. The world's greatest salespeople don't "appear" to be selling anything at all. In fact, you'll never catch a great salesperson making any *irritating* sales pitches or initiating a single close.

2. Despite the fact that the world's greatest salespeople don't appear to be selling anything, they still manage to outsell every one of their competitors![1]

Now, think about it: Do you really believe that Steve Jobs became one of the most beloved CEOs in the world using "old school" forms of subtle persuasion? Or what about Mary Kay Ash? Can you imagine her using "leading questions" on national TV? Of course not!

The world's greatest salespeople are the people most admired by everyone you know. They interact with thousands (and even millions) of people each year. They make the most money, attract the most opportunities, and rise effortlessly to the top of every profession.

And I promise you this: You'll never catch them in the "act" of selling!

The fact is that the world's best salespeople are so good, they don't seem to be doing *anything* the traditional sales training experts teach. And what exactly do traditional sales training experts teach? They teach *how to sell* instead of *why people buy*.

If you remember anything from this book, remember this: People love to buy, but they hate to be sold to. I first learned this from legendary marketing guru Freeman Gosden. He said, "If I can tell you one thing: Remember that it's not what and how you sell something that's important, it's what and how your customer wishes to buy that's important."

And that's why I teach this simple motto in all my seminars: *In order to sell more, you must first learn to sell less, a whole lot less.*

Sound crazy?

Well, it is a crazy—*but it works!*

A good friend of mine moved from selling photocopier machines to selling Mercedes-Benzes in the most prestigious dealership in New England. His secret? While selling photocopiers, he did the exact opposite of what everyone else in his company was doing: He focused less on selling and more on why his customers wanted to buy; he stopped selling altogether and made it his mission to discover precisely how he could solve more problems for his customers than anyone else in his company. He not only solved more problems, but he made more money and opened up more opportunities than any other copier "salesman" in his industry.

Selling Less = More Sales

I've spent thirty years and countless thousands of dollars studying all the best sales courses I could get my hands on. I read all the books, listened to all the tape programs, and attended many seminars. I studied each program like a detective, methodically pulling out the best techniques from each system and applying them immediately to every situation I could imagine.

The more I studied these programs and practiced the various techniques, the more frustrated I became. Nothing I found seemed to work well in the real world! In fact, most sales training programs aren't designed to work!

If you need proof, try using a fancy closing technique on one of your kids, or "information gathering" with your spouse. If you can't get away with those so-called skills with the people you love the most, why on earth would you use them with your customers? Yet, that's precisely what most salespeople do.

They employ manipulative strategies and "techniques" on their customers that they wouldn't dare use on their families and friends.

And if that's not bad enough, in a recent Gallup poll on the *honesty* and *ethical conduct* of business professionals, insurance and car salespeople were ranked at the bottom of the list!

Now, you shouldn't be too surprised to hear this. Bill Brooks of the Brooks Group estimates that more than 85 percent of customers have a negative view of salespeople. And Richard Bradshaw, president of the National Association of Purchasing Management, says, "Unprepared, dishonest, pushy, and lazy reps are too common to count." And commission-crazed managers are often the reason, forcing reps into 'drive-by selling,' as one rep calls it—quick and easy deals rather than customer-focused relationships."[2]

Most people—whether we want to believe it or not—are smart.

They are not fooled by old school sales techniques. It doesn't matter how clever or disguised you think these kinds of behaviors are. Traditional sales methods send up an immediate red flag in the mind of almost every prospect you see.

You probably know yourself when you're being manipulated or lied to by a salesperson. Most people have a sixth sense for this kind of treatment. Some sales professionals think they can fool their prospects with charm, flattery, and dramatic appeal, but these behaviors only mask the underlying motivation behind every word the salesperson utters.

Yesterday's sales training no longer applies to today's fast-paced environment. What worked for your predecessors won't work for you today.

What have you done to prepare yourself for this insanely competitive environment? Have you been to any sales training seminars? Read any books on the subject? And if so, how current was the technology in your training? How "cutting edge" and timely were the strategies in your books? Has the material been consistently tested in real-world situations?

Throughout this book are short exercises for you to do on your own to track your progress and to help you become more and more comfortable and confident with your new skills. As you read, you'll want to have paper and pen ready to write notes (even directly in the book) as ideas come to mind.

If you are looking for remedies, techniques, suggestions, solutions, and genuine help in understanding the art of good salesmanship, then you have come to the right place.

If you are looking for a quick, "down and dirty" answer that tells you exactly what to say, word for word, for every sales scenario you will face, then I suggest you read other books on selling.

My purpose in writing this book is to help you awaken the areas of your personality that can help you become more successful, both professionally and personally. You will learn how to uncover areas in your thinking and acting that prevent you from tapping into your full sales potential.

The world is full of books on sales tactics that tell you to memorize "mistakes." They also create scenarios that give you specific language to use for every sales situation. They pump you up with affirmation statements and teach you how to magically transform a prospect's no into a yes in minutes. If that's what you want, then you are reading the wrong book. Close this book right now, find your receipt, and return it to the bookstore immediately.

If, however, you would like to tap into that part of you that truly wants to learn how to master the art of good communication and salesmanship, then keep on reading. The key to this book is in understanding that you must "tap into" your own inner sales greatness. Being a successful salesperson has more to do with you than with the sales process itself.

---

[1] Most people don't think of successful business executives and celebrities as salespeople. In fact, when most of us think of a typical salesperson, we think of a pushy used car salesman or an annoying insurance rep. But these so-called "salespeople" aren't really salespeople at all; they're professional peddlers (cashiers in fancy suits).

[2] *Sales & Marketing Management* magazine, June 2001.

PART ONE
Getting Started

discovering the salesperson within

WHEN YOU THINK about your first professional sales job, the choices are so numerous that I could write another book just on that subject. I use the word *professional* because most people have already had a sales job while they were growing up. From a newspaper route, a lemonade stand, babysitting, or selling Girl Scout and Boy Scout cookies to fund-raising activities in elementary, junior, and senior high school.

Here is a short list of types of sales jobs and some examples of type of compensation:

- ✗ Sales clerk in a retail or department store, starting from $10/hour to $25,000 per year, plus possible commissions or bonus.

- ✗ Sales associate in insurance, real estate, mutual funds, or in a stock brokerage house, starting from $15/hour to $30,000 per year, plus possible bonuses.

- ✗ Inbound telemarketing, at $7–10/hour. People call into a center to buy or inquire about products or services.

- ✗ Outbound telemarketing, at $10–30/hour, plus bonus or commission. The telemarketer initiates calls to a list of prospects to sell a product or service.

- ✗ Sales trainee (with a college or graduate degree) for a corporation, $25,000–60,000/year plus bonus or commission.

- ✗ Stock broker or insurance agent, $15,000–40,000/first year, financing or start up salary with commission.

Then there are sales opportunities in network marketing or direct sales for those who wish to build a business or have a following or large contact base. There's no salary, but the investment to start up is usually less than $1,000.

Whatever job in sales you choose, in order to be reasonably successful—as well as feel happy and fulfilled—you'll need at the very least a set of tools and resources and a mindset for sales. By mindset, I mean the following:

1. The ability to communicate effectively, elegantly, and persuasively with different types of people from all walks of life, with different backgrounds and styles of communication. We cover this ability in depth in Chapter 7, called Step 2: Establishing Rapport.

2. The ability to ask open-ended questions and listen well (a conversation between two or more people). We cover this skill in Chapter 8. In the sales interview process, it's Step 3: Finding the Pain.

3. The ability to tell short, relevant stories that appeal to the prospect's needs and interests. We cover this in more detail in Chapter 12, entitled The Presentation.

4. The ability to see the glass as half full rather than half empty and then act accordingly. In other words, to be reasonably

positive and enthusiastic about your product, service, and most of all, yourself.

There are also several stages to sales success, each one leading to the next, with lots of lessons to be learned along the way. The following is a list of those stages and approximate timetables to enact them:

Stage 1: Start-up—the first ninety days on the job.
What to Do: Listen well, take notes, observe the actions and behavior of the top salespeople in the company; study and ask lots of questions.

Stage 2: Survival—the next nine months.
What to Do: Follow up all leads; make contacts; learn from the top sales leaders and always ask for advice and help.

Stage 3: Growth—from one to three years.
What to Do: While your client base, revenues, and resources are all growing, learn from your mistakes and adapt to the changes that occur.

Stage 4: Expansion—from three to six years.
What to Do: Get much better at delegating and being organized. You then have the right systems in place and working, including your business, sales, and marketing plan.

Stage 5: Maturity—somewhere between six and ten years.
What to Do: Very little! All systems, resources, and profit centers are practically running on autopilot, and you are enjoying the fruits of your labor.

Stage 6: Exit—whenever you're ready to retire and enjoy the benefits of your "successful sales career" or change careers and do something else you love.

Now, let's discover the salesperson within you!

Here's a true story:

Two young men spent an evening telemarketing for a newspaper. They both called prospects from the same list, using the same script, selling the same product for the same price, yet one man sold nothing and managed to offend almost every person he spoke with, whereas the other man outsold everyone else in his department and had some of the most rewarding conversations of his life.

What is the difference between these two men, and how could their similar behaviors produce such diametrically opposed results?

PRESCRIPTION FOR SUCCESS

The secret to successful selling doesn't come from any fancy "sales technique" or a complicated theory in a book; the secret to successful selling comes from inside you.

You have everything it takes to be a truly successful salesperson, but it's trapped within you.

In fact, I believe that most people are born salespeople. Just observe the first few years of childhood: *Did you ever notice how many times children keep asking for what they want?* They can go on forever.

Most children have no fear of rejection or ridicule in asking for what they want. How often do we get one "no" or a "maybe" and hang our heads in shame thinking, "I'm a terrible salesperson." I've got news for you: There are no terrible salespeople. There are only *untrained* individuals who haven't consistently implemented the kinds of powerful selling tools that thousands of successful salespeople use daily in their professional lives. This book helps you cultivate those tools for yourself and translate them into a dynamic selling language that everyone understands and to which people can respond.

Exercise 1: Self-Inventory—Unleashing the Salesperson Within

Get a piece of paper and fold it in half. While standing in front of a mirror with this book and a pen in hand, take sixty seconds to stare in the mirror at yourself and record what you see. For example, "I'm five feet, eleven inches. I have black hair and blue eyes." Like that.

Next, stare into the mirror again, but this time record what you *can't* see with your eyes, but which you know is there. (For example, are you easygoing or hard to get along with? Are you introverted or extroverted? Patient or impatient?)

Take several minutes to do this portion of the exercise. Put a lot of thought into it. No one will see your responses unless you share them, so be honest with yourself about the things that you *don't* see.

EXERCISE EVALUATION

Something you may have noticed:

Your outside descriptions are probably quite different from your inside descriptions.

In fact, who you are on the inside, the part you don't see, affects everything about you, your job, your relationships, and your overall satisfaction with your life.

Think about it: How much more time do we spend cultivating ourselves from the outside, thinking, "If only I drove a better car, or had a better briefcase, or a more impressive wardrobe . . . then I'd be perceived as a more successful executive and get more sales!" Or as Willie Loman suggested in Arthur Miller's play *Death of a Salesman*, "You only need to be well liked." But again, these are only external qualities, and external qualities rarely determine one's sales success.

Perhaps you've heard the old saw about the self-made millionaire stripped of all the outward signs of her wealth:

Find a self-made millionaire sales executive earning a few hundred thousand dollars per year. Take away her job, contacts, home, and expensive clothing, and move her to a strange city where she doesn't know anyone at all. Then there's the question: Where will this sales executive be in another five years?

If she implements the same principles that made her rich the first time, she'll most likely be in the same position she was before everything was taken away. In fact, 99.999 percent of sales success is an inside job; it has more to do with you as a *person* than you as a *personality*.

We've all seen the personality-oriented car peddlers using the old shuck-and-jive pitching techniques, flashing their business cards and phony smiles. These characters have become an American cliché, like apple pie and baseball, although without the respect. Unfortunately, personality-oriented salespeople don't produce many sales. They exert a great deal of external effort into their professions but end up with little or no payoff in the end.

Exercise 2: Self-Assessment

Do you have what it takes to unleash your "inner salesperson"? Take this short self-assessment test and find out now.

Instructions: Find someplace where you won't be disturbed for at least ten minutes. Take out a pen and circle the appropriate response to each of the questions on the following pages.

Note: Don't think too much about your answers; circle whichever response occurs to you first.

1. I provide abundant details about matters I think are important, regardless of whether my listeners agree with me.
   A. Frequently
   B. On occasion
   C. I've never noticed
   D. Never

2. I say things that sound surprising, confusing, or strange simply to grab attention.
A. Whenever necessary
B. Rarely, if at all
C. I've never noticed
D. Never

3. When I speak with another person, I tend to use the person's name often.
A. Always
B. Sometimes
C. I've never noticed
D. Not at all

4. I tend to speak in run-on sentences, quickly stating connections and parallels between facts and ideas.
A. Never
B. Rarely
C. On occasion
D. Frequently

5. I tell stories and illustrate my points with metaphors, anecdotes, and analogies.
A. Never
B. Rarely
C. On occasion
D. Frequently

6. When I speak with others, I often use words like "must," "have to," and "should."
A. Usually
B. Sometimes
C. I've never noticed
D. Rarely

7. When a friend or colleague feels down, I try to be cheerful to bring the other person out of the doldrums.
   A. Usually
   B. Some of the time
   C. Depends on how I feel
   D. Hardly ever

8. If someone at work has an objection to what I say or propose, the first thing I do is restate my position.
   A. Most of the time
   B. Sounds like a good idea
   C. Sometimes
   D. Rarely

9. In listening situations, I frequently restate what I've heard with phrases such as, "as I understand it, you mean."
   A. Most of the time
   B. On occasion
   C. Rarely
   D. Hardly ever

10. If another person in an exchange stops speaking, I immediately break the silence.
   A. Most of the time
   B. Frequently
   C. On occasion
   D. Rarely

SCORING YOURSELF

For questions 1, 4, 5, 6, 7, 8 and 10, give yourself four points for D, three for C, two for B, and one for A. For questions 2, 3, and 9 give yourself four points for A, three for B, two for C, and one for D.

34 or above: You're a master at winning others over. You possess fine influencing skills and feel comfortable using them.

33 to 28: Though not a star in persuasion, you have good skills. Choose a skill to practice and make it a permanent part of your "influence inventory."

27 to 22: You're on your way. Practice persuasive behavior one point at a time during your routine.

21 or below: Listening attentively to others and grasping how they feel helps you motivate them more effectively. Improving your own persuasive powers enables you to overcome self-consciousness.

Exercise 3: Self-Inventory
PART 1: ASSESSING YOUR PERSONAL AND PROFESSIONAL STRENGTHS

In this section, I want you to make a list of your strengths. An example of this might be:

Mental Strengths

I have a good, fertile imagination.

I enjoy learning new skills.

I'm very patient.

I have a willingness to exert great effort in my job.

Emotional Strengths

I'm very receptive to other people.

I have an objective perspective on everybody around me.

I'm enthusiastic about my job.

I'm ambitious.

I'm curious about learning new things.

Physical Strengths

My body is strong and healthy.

I've got an upright, sturdy posture.

I have clear, powerful speech.

I look good.

Professional Strengths

I have the ability to manage well.

I have the ability to motivate others

I can easily create rapport with my prospects.

I'm a good listener.

I possess good questioning skills.

PART 2: ASSESSING YOUR PERSONAL AND PROFESSIONAL WEAKNESSES

In this section, make a list of your weaknesses. An example of this might be:

Personal Weaknesses

Poor selling skills

Poor work ethic

Laziness

Procrastination

Poor time management

Personal Liabilities

Bad marriage

Financial debts

Draining relationships

Serious illness

Disabilities

Professional Liabilities

Unhappy job

Disrespectful or unethical employees or colleagues

After you've listed your personal and professional strengths and weaknesses above, simply go down your list and next to each entry write an "I" for internal or an "E" for external. For example, next to your entry "I look good," you'd write an "E" for external, because good looks can be taken away or modified by some outside force, such as old age or a skin rash. Next to your entry "I'm very receptive to other people," you'd write an "I" for internal, because unlike good looks, being receptive to other people is not as easily taken away or modified by something or someone outside yourself.

After labeling your various entries, notice whether you wrote more external than internal strengths.

The world's most powerful, successful sales professionals work and live *exclusively* from their *internal* strengths. In other words, if you took away the external strength from an internally oriented sales professional, that person would most likely continue producing an ongoing string of successful personal and professional ventures. Look at Christopher Reeves or Michael J. Fox as two outstanding examples of men who've had many external strengths taken away but who still manage just fine on all the internal strengths they've built throughout the course of their lives.

If your external strengths far outnumber your internal strengths, there are many things you can do to reorient yourself as an internally driven sales professional:

1. Create a higher purpose for your career. When we get to the goal-setting chapter, Chapter 2, be sure to take a lot of time examining your "higher purpose" when it comes to selling. Often we simply fall into a sales career as a last-ditch effort to pay bills or make ends meet. Examining what you truly want out of your career helps you *own* your decision to become a true master of sales success.

2. Take responsibility for everything that happens to you on the job. Getting a lot of bad leads this week? Don't go hounding your sales manager for better contacts; instead, take a proactive approach and look for some leads on your own. (Check out the list in Chapter 18, titled "Twenty-Five Low Cost Ways to Attract New Prospects and Clients Without Having to Cold Call" for more information on lead generation tactics and strategies.)

3. Develop a daily meditation practice. The main cause of most mental and physical illnesses is energy imbalance in the body. Meditation helps you return to your perfectly balanced state by cultivating positive and peaceful states of mind, thus reducing stress and other negative states of mind until they are eventually eradicated altogether. By engaging in a regular meditation practice, you will live a longer, healthier life—not to mention having less stress on the job. An excellent book for beginner's meditation is *Transform Your Life* (2001) by Geshe Kelsang Gyatso.

Chapter 1 Summary

Sales Fact: The world's most powerful, successful sales professionals work and live *exclusively* from their *internal* strengths.

- ✗ The secret to successful selling doesn't come from some fancy sales technique or a complicated theory in a book; the secret to successful selling comes from *inside* you.

- ✗ You have everything it takes to be a truly successful salesperson, but it's trapped within you.

- ✗ 99.999 percent of sales success is an inside job; success has to do more with you *as a person* than you as a personality.

Things you can do to reorient yourself as an internally driven sales professional:

1. Create a higher purpose for your career.

2. Take responsibility for everything that happens to you on the job.

3. Develop a daily meditation practice.

2

creating a "go" plan of action

HAVING GOALS allows us to make life an enjoyable game and helps us to focus on the specific direction that we want to take. Many people set their goals in stone and carry them around as a burden. Others take goals so lightly that they never accomplish anything at all. Goals are like a road map for personal and professional growth, evolving and changing as we continue through life. With well-planned goals, we are always in a position of "arriving" rather than one of "having arrived."

Most people do not set goals. They have "an idea" or they have their goals "in mind." People who do not set goals are like travelers in a strange land without a destination. They just drift from place to place without any direction or sense of accomplishment. As sales and motivational expert Zig Ziglar says, "People without goals are wandering generalities as opposed to being meaningful specifics."

A clear example of the value of goal-setting comes out of a study done on the Yale University class of 1953. At commencement, the graduates were asked if they had written clear, specific goals. Only 3 percent had. Twenty years later, the researchers went back and interviewed the surviving members. They discovered that the 3 percent who had written specific goals were worth more financially than the other 97 percent put together.

PRESCRIPTION FOR SUCCESS

Ask bold, imaginative questions of life, and some of your answers may turn out wrong. Ask puny, insignificant questions, and it won't matter if your answers are right. No one will care.

So where do you begin? Begin with the end in mind. Start by asking yourself some basic questions, such as, "What do I want out of life?" "How much money do I want?" "What kind of relationships do I want?" "What kind of work gets me really fired up?" If you can't think of anything or you're telling yourself that it really doesn't matter, STOP! Take a minute to recognize that these thoughts are barriers that you put between yourself and success.

The Magic Wand Exercise

Lie down and relax. Play some soft music in the background. Pretend that you were given a magic wand and 10 million dollars, tax free! You are then sent on a six-month vacation around the world, first class all the way. You are now back home, and you still have the 10 million dollars and the magic wand you can use to create any opportunities you desire. What will you do? Where will you live? Now project yourself five years into the future. Picture yourself sitting in the favorite room of your favorite home.

Where is it? What room is it? What does it look like? Put as much detail in the picture as you can. What does the wallpaper look like? When you look out the window, what do you see? There are two pictures in this room. One is of your family and one is of your friends.

Imagine the faces in the pictures. Do you recognize them? Maybe you can't put faces on the people. How many people do you see? There is an appointment book there. Look through it. What kinds of appointments and activities do you have scheduled? What is your normal day like? Whom do you spend your time with? What are you doing? What charities are you working with? Picture yourself sitting in your favorite chair. Now as you look around the room, feeling very comfortable and relaxed, you begin to reflect on the past five years. What have you done? One thing comes to mind that you have done or are still doing that you feel particularly proud of. What is it? Picture yourself telling someone you respect highly about this thing. Feel the way you would feel saying, "I did it!" Now think about what the next five years will bring. What things do you still have to do? Enjoy sitting in this chair, reflecting, dreaming, and experiencing as long as you like, and know that you can come back to it anytime you want.

After you get up, write down everything you can remember. Try to get as much detail in the description as you possibly can. You can do this exercise again and again. You may change everything or just add more detail to the same situation. The important thing is to write it down each time. Eventually, you will notice patterns and be able to formulate goals. Don't be surprised if the things you dream wouldn't cost nearly 10 million dollars. This is very common. The point to understand is that even your wildest dreams are probably not that extravagant. They are certainly attainable, so why not allow yourself to dream? You can do it.

PRESCRIPTION FOR SUCCESS

Limited goals can create limited lives, so stretch yourself as far as you can in setting your goals.

Review your goals on a regular basis. Seeing them in your mind accelerates the process of achieving them. Your mind does whatever you program it to do. Your unconscious mind is constantly processing information in ways that move you in particular directions. Make sure that you are setting the direction consciously.

Rules for Writing Goals

1. State your goals as positive affirmations in the present tense. As you write each goal in the present affirmative, you are acting as if the goal is already achieved. Developing a goal in this manner makes it appear more vivid and more possible.

   Example: "I am sitting in the living room of the new home that I just purchased," or, "I have just closed the ABC account with an order for 10,000 units."

2. Be as specific as possible. How does your goal look, sound, feel, and smell? Use all your senses in describing it.

3. Do a "reality check." Know how you are looking and feeling and what you are hearing as you achieve your goal. You can be winning and still feel like you are losing if you don't keep score.

4. Be in control. Your goal must be controlled by you; it cannot depend on others changing themselves to make you happy.

5. Be sure that your goal is ethically and ecologically sound and *desirable*. Would you want to see it in front-page headlines? Consider whom it affects and what consequences you will have to live with.

6. Avoid having to have *only* the desired goal. When you feel that you must have something, you automatically energize its opposite by resisting it. For best results, be willing to let conditions that you might not understand manifest themselves. Then go ahead and enthusiastically reaffirm your goal.

The following pages provide you with a format for writing your goals. Write at least one goal for each time frame. Be sure to use the present affirmative and be as specific as possible.

Make a Goal Ledger

You can keep account of a broad spectrum of goals by maintaining a ledger. Here are eleven tips:

1. Begin by writing your goals down.

2. Next to each goal, indicate its importance (V = very important; M = moderately important; L = least important).

3. Indicate whether any given goal conflicts with another goal. If this is the case, determine which goal is a priority and whether alternatives and adjustments can be made.

4. Some of your goals may fall under the following topics: career satisfaction; salaries, bonuses, and extracurricular earnings; learning and education; status and respect; other.

5. Now that you have written out some goals for the next ten years, go back and assign them time frames (a week, month, six months, one year, five years, ten years). Then choose the highest priority goal in each category and circle it.

6. Take one of the goals you circled and write down how you know when you have achieved it absolutely. Be clear and specific. Write down why you're sure you did it and why it was important to you. Remember to use both the present and past tense.

7. Make a list of all the important resources you have at your disposal. This list should include your character traits, friends, financial resources, education, and talents.

8. In order to re-create positive energy, focus on a time in your life when you used your resources most successfully. Find a time when you felt totally successful. It could be a business

deal, sports, a relationship, or a great day with your family. Describe what you did that made you succeed and why you felt successful.

9. Now, thinking in the past tense about the goal at hand, describe the kind of person you had to be to attain this goal. Did you have to be more disciplined? Did you need more education? Better time management? Write a couple of paragraphs about the character traits, skills, attitudes, beliefs, and disciplines that you needed to achieve the desired result.

10. Again, in the past tense, create your first draft of a step-by-step plan on how you achieved your goal. Ask yourself, "What did I have to do first to accomplish that?" Then, in the present tense, make a list of what you need to do today.

11. Make a list of all the things in your life that you already have that were once goals or dreams. Acknowledge the obstacles you've overcome, the people you are most grateful to, and the resources that you have available. Develop an "attitude of gratitude."

It is important that you take time to make a written journal, or ledger, of your goals. It may not be easy at first, but as you begin to go through the process, your goals will become more vivid and believable. Success comes from hard work and a clear intention.

Single Out a Major Goal

As specifically as possible, state the major goal for which you are striving, then answer these six questions:

1. How important is it that I achieve this goal?

2. How does this goal relate to my long-term goals? Are there conflicts?

3. What will happen if I succeed?

4. What will happen if I fail?

5. How will I feel if I attain this goal?

6. How will I feel if I do not attain this goal?

HURDLES AND HELPS

One way to overcome our limitations is to know exactly what they are. Take a moment to write down all the reasons why you haven't yet achieved this goal. What causes or prevents you from having what you desire? Do you fail to plan? Do you have trouble getting people to buy into your ideas? Do you have too many irons in the fire? We all have ways that we limit ourselves. When we don't have the results that we desire, we usually have "reasons why." Discover yours now.

After you have defined your goal and have planned how to attain it, examine factors that can prevent you from achieving your goal (1 and 2), and steps you can take to reach it (3 and 4).

Step 1: List personal shortcomings to overcome and what you can do about them.

Step 2: List obstacles to overcome and what you can do about them.

Step 3: State the actions you need to take to achieve your goal.

Step 4: State what help and support you need to solicit from others.

PRESCRIPTION FOR SUCCESS

Reward yourself for specific achievements.

Tools for Success

1. Make a wish board. Collect pictures of things that represent your goals from magazines, brochures, etc., and paste them onto a large piece of posterboard. Even try to get photographs of yourself already in possession of the thing that you desire. Hang your wish board up in a place where it can be seen frequently. It can be your office, your kitchen, bedroom, or bathroom. This creates a visual reminder that will help reinforce your desire and keep you motivated.

2. Make your own subliminal tape. Tape record yourself repeating your positive goal affirmations over and over again in the present tense. Use a different tone and tempo each time. Have some music you like playing in the background. If you're not sure, use Baroque music; it has been proven to stimulate the learning process. Get an auto-reverse cassette player and play the tape softly as background music and throughout your day or while you sleep. It can be played at a barely audible level and still have a positive effect.

3. Make yourself a goal card. Write your goal on a 3" x 5" card. Above that write a date by which time you commit to achieving this goal. Below your goal, sign your name. For example, a goal card might read: "By October 31, 2004, I will have finished writing an article about sales success that will be published in a national magazine. Signed, F. Scott Fitzberry." Then carry this card around with you everywhere you go—in your wallet, your pocket, or your purse. As many times during the day as you can, pull the card out and read it. It could be in the elevator, standing in line, at a traffic light, or anytime else.

Especially be sure to read the card as soon as you wake up in the morning and just before you go to bed at night. It's not necessary that you let anyone else read your card. Their lack of understanding could cause embarrassment and harm your motivation. You will be amazed at how this works. You could write something you know to be untrue on the card, but if read enough times, it becomes believable. So that you can see how it works, make your first goal card a goal that won't take more than 30 to 60 days to reach. Remember to be positive and have fun with this wonderful new gift.

Your Plan of Action

Now that you have a good understanding of your higher purpose and a clear direction or set of goals, you have to get organized and formulate a plan of action. Even if organization is not your strong point, it's important to put together a system you can work with in order to keep track of the large quantity of leads and information you will be gathering. It's not difficult or complicated, and once you get used to it, you might even like it. The process of gathering information alone is of no benefit unless you are able to organize it intelligently and retrieve it. The simple system provided throughout this book is designed to do just that.

Why People Do Not Set Goals

1. They're not serious: just words—no action. They need to reverse that—to *action*, not just words.

2. They don't accept responsibility for their lives. They're still waiting for real life to just "happen," "waiting for their ship to come in," always waiting for a more convenient time. It's like buying a lottery ticket, always hoping for that lucky break.

3. They were raised in a negative atmosphere. "Can't" is the attitude of the household. "Oh, you can't do that." "Why do you think you're good enough to do that?"

4. They don't really understand or realize the importance of planning and setting goals.

5. They don't know how.

6. They fear criticism; they fear being ridiculed when trying to rise above the norm. They also fear sharing goals with others, which helps doom their success. (What we need is an association of people who understand the importance of goal-setting and who help each other reach their goals.)

7. They fear failure. This is the greatest deterrent and keeps people in their "comfort zone." They are already successful, so there's little chance for failure. But living this way doesn't teach any lessons; it doesn't stretch them to find out what they are really capable of accomplishing.

PRESCRIPTION FOR SUCCESS

Fail forward fast; get all the "failures" out of the way as soon as possible.

Chapter 2 Summary

1. State your goals as positive affirmations in the present tense.

2. Be as specific as possible.

3. Do a "reality check."

4. Be in control.

5. Be sure that your goal is ethically and ecologically sound and desirable.

6. Avoid having to have *only* the desired goal.

The wise individual understands that *failure* isn't failure at all; it's a lesson, a temporary glitch on the way to accomplishing a goal.

3

finding the right job

MY GRANDFATHER once told me a story about a wise old leader in an ancient village. Often, during village council meetings, people would come to him with serious problems and he would always come up with the right answers. There was a precocious, arrogant young man who wanted to be the new leader. He thought that if he could just trick the old man and put him into a no-win situation, he would be the smart one. He found a baby chick and cupped it in both his hands with his thumb and forefinger around its neck. His plan was to go to the wise man and ask him if the chick in his hands was alive or dead. If the man said it was alive, he would twist its neck and it would be dead. If the man said it was dead, he'd open his hands and show him it was alive. He really had him now.

At the next council meeting, the young man approached the leader with the chick inside his hands. "Oh, wise leader, I have a baby chick inside my hands. Is it alive or dead?"

The elder leader paused and gave thought. After a short while, the young man spoke again. "Tell me, leader, is this chick alive or dead? You have all the answers!" The wise leader looked directly into the young man's eyes and said: "No, my young friend. You do. It is your choice. It is whatever you truly want it to be."

And so it can be with your job search—it can be anything you want it to be.

In fact, no matter how bad the economy is doing, you can still attract the job of your dreams—easily and without frustration. Finding the right sales job needn't be a burdensome, overwhelming experience for the serious professional. If you follow a few simple guidelines, you'll not only place yourself ahead of 99 percent of your competition, but you'll also find your job search to be faster and more enjoyable than you ever thought possible.

The Six Guidelines for Finding the Right Job

1. Your first task in finding a job is to make finding a job your job. In other words, you need to be up, dressed, and ready for work each morning by 9:00 a.m. *sharp*—just as if you had a position to fill at an office (that means no sleeping in till noon and casually peeking through the classifieds over a roast beef sandwich at lunch).

2. You need to work a full eight-hour day (with a lunch break, of course).

3. You need to be dressed *professionally*, in the clothing appropriate to the position you're seeking (that means no making phone calls in your boxer shorts and bathrobe).

4. You need a quiet area of your house or apartment from where you do most of your work. *Hint:* Avoid rooms with televisions, radios, magazines, and computer games. You wouldn't have those distractions in an office, and you don't need them for your job search either.

5. You need to have a place to work with a desk (or kitchen table), telephone, fax machine, paper and pens, and computer. If you don't have a computer, don't worry. Most local libraries can supply this valuable tool.

6. You also need to have a to-do list of job-seeking activities that you've itemized and arranged the previous night.

You may be wondering, "Why all the fuss?" Do we really need all this preparation, rules, and regimentation? Why can't we take it easy and make a few calls in our leisure time throughout the day?

The answer is that a leisurely approach to a job search gets you mediocre results at best. You need to treat your search like a miner searching for gold—because a right-fitting sales job can be worth hundreds of thousands of dollars over the course of your selling career.

Finding the Perfect Fit—Know Something About Yourself

There are many different kinds of sales careers: inbound, retail, distribution, telemarketing, corporate, etc. Depending on your personality type, you will be more suited for one kind of job over another. For instance, a highly introverted personality may have great difficulty in a retail or corporate sales job; however, telemarketing sales might be just the right fit.

✗ *Introverted Personality:* The introvert directs thoughts and feelings *inward* and is often shy or reserved. Sales careers for introverts include, but are not limited to: inbound telemarketing, business-to-business, inside, and technical sales.

✗ *Extroverted Personality:* The extrovert directs attention toward other people and is usually outgoing, assertive, and highly responsive. Sales careers for extroverts include, but are not limited to: outbound telemarketing, business-to-consumer, retail, and door-to-door type selling.

Finding the Perfect Fit—Applying the 10-Step Job Interview to Prospective Employers

To get the right job and to take control of the job interview process, you need to treat the employment interview as if it's a "sales interview." The only difference is you're selling *yourself* as the product as opposed to selling a tangible product or service. In fact, the best salespeople are always selling themselves first. For more detailed information on each of the steps of the job interview, see the sales interview section that follows in Part 2.

WHERE YOU BEGIN

The first place most people go to find a job is the classifieds ads. But contrary to popular belief, classified ads, including Internet searches, are not always the best place to find the best jobs; they are the place to find leads and to do research to see what kinds of jobs are available.

Fact: Most employers (more than 70 percent) are more likely to hire an applicant that they already know—or is an associate of somebody they know—than an unfamiliar applicant who sends in a résumé and cover letter. That's why sending a résumé and cover letter in response to a classified ad is one of the least effective ways to build a relationship with a prospective employer.

Success Tip: Go to your local library, get back issues of *Selling Power, Entrepreneur,* and *Inc.* and research the top 500 sales companies in your immediate area. Look for companies that really interest you, the kinds of places you'd pay to work in. Once you've found five or six companies that meet these criteria, you're ready to move to *Step 1* of the Job Interview Process:

Step 1: Pre-Call Planning. This is where you find out everything about the company or companies that you wish to pursue by researching them in the business and trade journals, business reference books, directories in your local library, and, especially, the Internet. You can usually learn a great deal from the company's Web site, including the degree of professionalism and quality of the company's products and services. Find out who the founder or owner was, the current president, VP of sales, and the sales manager for the territory you're interested in. You might even call the company directly and ask for the personal assistant, president, or owner, or in some cases, the media department, to find out specifically what they sell, how many employees they have, and how long they've been in business. Jot down notes on the various points of interest that excite you. After you've done this, you simply call up the person in charge of the department you want to work in and request an information or exploratory interview.

Step 2: Interviewing the Interviewer. When you go to the recruiter, sales manager, or owner, in order to establish rapport early on, you need to interview them. For example, begin your interview by saying: "Mr./Ms. Employer, before we begin the formal interview, may I ask you a few questions? To what do you attribute your own success, as well as the success of your company?" Only after you've gotten them to talk a bit about themselves and their company do you move on to Step 3.

Step 3: Asking Specific Questions. You then ask the person specific questions about the job. For instance: "I've already done some preliminary research on your company, but I'd like to know a little more about how this position became available?" or "How long has the job been in existence?" "Is it a newly created position?" "What are the specific duties?" The purpose of these questions is to give you sufficient information about what the position entails and also to get the interviewer talking as much as possible—while you're taking notes.

Step 4: Establishing a Budget. In other words, inquire about the specific salary and compensation plan if you deliver the desired results.

Step 5: Decision-Making Process. What is the decision-making process for this position and who else besides yourself will be involved in the process? Are there any other decision makers you need to know about? This is where you find out whether or not you need to do a second interview with another person. Here you can ask: "Am I the first to be interviewed? How many others do you expect to interview? When do you expect to make a final decision?"

Up until this point, the employer has been talking about 80 percent of the time, and you're asking questions, taking notes, and learning a lot of valuable information.

Note: If a sales manager, recruiter, owner, or someone else to whom you're speaking stops you from going through this process, you need to gently say: "Mr./Ms. Employer, do you want the person you hire to sell for you to be able to establish *rapport* with prospects, find out specifically what they want and need, and help them get it, or would you rather have them just 'sell and tell'?" If they say no, they want them to sell and tell, then this is obviously not the most ideal sales job for you. They have, in effect, disqualified themselves from the interview. Remember, your job is to find and qualify the right job, with the right management and the right company. This is the same sales interview system you will use to sell your products, services, and, ultimately, yourself to your prospects.

Step 6: Reviewing. Examine everything that's been said thus far. For example: "Mr./Ms. Employer, I'd like to review the X, Y, and Z that you presented about this job and what your expectations are." When you've finished going through each point, you then ask: "Do I understand that correctly?"

Step 7: Confirming. If the employer says yes to Step 6, you're now in an excellent position to present your reasons why you'd be perfect for the job. And, obviously, you know why you're perfect for the job because they just told you what they're looking for.

Success Tip: Present two out of three or three out of five of your matched skills, talents, and abilities for the job available (check with the interviewers after each skill is presented to make sure they agree that it fits what they're looking for) and then stop. You're ready for Step 8.

Step 8: Evaluating Your Status. "Mr. Employer, I still have a few more things I could present to you, but if you will give me an idea about where we stand right now—with zero being that you have no interest in me and ten that you already see me working as a vital part of your team, delivering what you want, the way you want it—where would you say we are right now?"

Note: If it's anything below a 5, ask, "Gee, can you help me out here? What did I leave out or miss for me not to have a higher score?" If it's a 6 or above: "What would we need to cover for us to be at a 10?" You then specifically address each point until you get to 10. If they've said 10, guess what? The sale is closed; you got the job! Don't oversell yourself. Your only response should be: "What do we need to do to finalize this?" (which is Step 9).

Step 9: The Close. Here's where you ask: "Mr./Ms. Employer, Now that we're a 10, when do you see me starting?" If the employer says, "I need to talk to so-and-so first," you say, "Let's pretend you are the sole person who makes this decision. If it were up to you, would *you* hire me?"

Note: This is a reaffirmation that they want to hire you and will fight for you, if necessary. When you've established the employer's willingness to hire you, you are ready for Step 10.

Step 10: The After-Close. Find out how you can have an outstanding first day, first week, and first month on the job by asking the following questions: "What tips or mentoring could you share with me to make me ready for my first day on the job? How can I best be prepared for working successfully as a vital part of your team?"

WHAT DO YOU SAY OR DO IF YOU DO NOT WANT THE JOB?

If you know you don't want this job, you say: "I'm not sure this is a perfect fit and I need to get back to you. Is it okay if I find someone who's a better fit and refer them to you?" Be graceful and cordial in declining the job, because if things change, you may want to come back in the future. Also, it's better to admit up front that you don't want the job than simply to take it for the money—and be miserable.

Interview Questions for Your Prospective Boss

Your relationship and communication with your next boss will probably have more to do with your success than any other single job-related factor. You need to know how your boss handles expectations, goals, disagreements, successes, mistakes, priorities, risk, reports, decisions, negotiations, anger, and conflict. Once you know your prospective boss's style, you must compare that with your style and decide if you are compatible.

Your prospective boss's responses to the following questions will tell you a lot. Take notes, not of your boss's words alone, but of what comes across to you—anxiety, patience, interest, anger, etc.—from body language, vocal variations, facial expressions, and all the other clues you can get.

1. What is your number-one priority in the next six months? (Get specifics here; "Better than we did last year" isn't specific. "A 12 percent increase in our glass product's market share" is.)

2. What specific results would you expect of me over the next six months? (Again, get as specific as you can. If it can't be measured, there could a question as to whether you achieved it.)

3. How do you define a top performer? (Is it realistic, doable, or challenging? Does it fit you?)

4. How do you plan to measure my productivity? (If there is no such plan, beware of traps. Suggest how you would like to be measured and note your boss's response.)

5. How will I know if my performance displeases you? (Beware of the boss who conceals displeasure or glosses over this question.)

6. How receptive are you to changes, innovations, trying out new ways of doing things? (If the boss has the "not invented here" attitude, expect the challenge in the job to be minimal.)

7. What level of decisions would you expect me to make? (Get specifics on dollars, resources, and authority.)

8. What should I do if I think you're making a mistake? (Pay close attention to the response to this one. Egomaniacs expect you to deny or ignore their mistakes.)

9. How will I know what your decisions are? (What you're really interested in here is how involved you will be in the decision-making process, and the response to this question should tell you.)

10. What is the negotiation period after you make a decision? Or, how should I approach you in negotiating a decision change? (The response to this one will give you a gauge to the boss's flexibility, reasonableness, and openness to input.)

11. How can I tell whether something is important to you? (In other words, how can you figure out the boss's priorities?)

12. How often would you want updates on my projects? (The "leash" should lengthen with time and trust.)

13. In what form do you prefer communications? (Spoken in person, spoken on the phone, written briefs, detailed written reports, e-mails? This is a critical one. Be sure you're comfortable with the answer.)

14. How do you expect satisfaction or appreciation to be expressed? (If your boss appears uncomfortable with this one, you might be facing a job in which your achievements go unacknowledged and unappreciated.)

15. How do you handle conflict? (If the reply is the equivalent of "openly and directly and immediately," that's great. If, on

the other hand, your boss denies the existence of conflict in the organization, run for the door.)

16. What should I do if you become angry? (A mature individual will respond with something reasonable, such as, "Just leave the room and let me finish blowing off steam—and give me the opportunity to apologize later." Any response that implies that you should endure verbal abuse in silence is unacceptable.)

17. Do you have any idiosyncrasies that I should know about? (Leaving early Tuesdays to play golf with some old cronies is one thing; standing on the conference table and berating people while stomping is quite another.)

18. What are the ground rules for calling you at home? (Make careful notes and follow them.)

19. About what moral or ethical issues do you have strong feelings? (Are these in sync with your own? Can you respect and accommodate them?)

20. What should I do if I think my work puts me in an ethical bind? (Suggestions that you should forget it won't work. You're after an invitation to have a serious discussion.)

21. Do you accept rough drafts or do you want everything in complete, final form?

22. How much do you want to know about a problem? (Full details, rough outline, bottom line, or something in between?)

23. What period of the day do you prefer to get information? (Whatever it is, prepare to respect it.)

Finding a Job Through Networks

What is a network? A network serves as a referral, introduction, and promotion system, with opportunities to support and help the individuals involved. It offers openings to establish and maintain relationships with people who can open up new ideas, contacts, and opportunities.

What is the purpose of belonging to a network? The purpose of a network is to help qualified, competent people in similar or related fields to have access to and a system to connect with other positive professionals and groups, creating a powerful resource bank.

Networks must be created, cultivated, and nurtured. They don't just happen. In the process of building your network, watch out for users and abusers—those people who tout their contacts or sources, promise you introductions, and usually, after you deliver the goods a few times, are too busy or just forget to "make good." An easy way to spot these people is to pay particular attention to their behavior, rather than listening to their words. If their behavior is not congruent with their language, it's crucial that you "close the file" on them quickly and get on with it.

More than *half* of the jobs you'll get in the course of your working life will come through people you already know. *Hint:* The more people you know, the easier time you'll have attracting the right sales position.

Here are the kinds of positive people you want as part of what I call your MasterMind network:

Cornerstones: People who form the foundation of your network and are necessary for your business, such as efficient and effective secretaries, competent administrative assistants, and reliable, trustworthy partners.

Internal Experts: People in your organization on whose talents and expertise you rely for data, research, factual statistics, and information.

External Experts: People in your field whom you respect, admire, and value as professional contacts and would easily recommend to others because of their integrity, reliability, and professional competence.

Related Experts: The same as above, except in related fields and whom you yourself might use to help get your job done, or people who can help your clients and prospects get their jobs done better: lawyers, accountants, printers, insurance specialists, etc.

Mentors: People who can help guide your career or business by providing opportunities to learn the ropes with a minimal amount of pain. They provide a forum for brainstorming and problem solving and also give you access to their power resources.

Role Models: People whose success, achievements, and professional behavior stimulate your own creative juices. They are the examples you want to emulate.

Power Sources: Those clients, prospects, or friends who refer you to additional sources of information and connections. They have the ability to get you qualified introductions.

Business Alliances: People in business who advise you of opportunities, encourage and promote your visibility with other businesses, and who work closely with you. (These might overlap with other categories.)

Challengers: People who do not yes you to death. They question you and test you to go the distance. They give you opportunities to look inside and find your own direction and face some important questions about your own life. While reminding you that you are a "ten," they press you on to improve your role performance, while giving you positive support along the way.

MasterMinds: A support group of like-minded positive professionals in similar or related industries, who meet on a regular basis, and assist each other in various ways. They may be drawn from any of the categories just listed.

PRESCRIPTION FOR SUCCESS

Building and maintaining professional sales networks is a life-long process.

Building a sales network is exactly like building a business. Once you are aware of the benefits, rewards, and satisfaction from these networks, you are on your way to realizing worthwhile, predetermined goals.

The Rules of Networking

1. Act like a host—not a guest. (Guests wait to be introduced. Hosts introduce themselves.)

2. Meet as many people as you can.

3. Don't spend more than five minutes with any one person. If there is interest, set follow-up appointments or call three to five days later.

4. Find out who they are, what they do, and what their market is.

5. Tell them what you do and what your market is.

6. Exchange business cards. Use the back of their card to note things such as where met, the date, and refresher notes, for example, three features or aspects of the person that struck you.

7. Do not do business while networking. (It is inappropriate and impractical. That's what follow-up appointments are for.)

8. Employ *give and get*. You must be able to do favors as well as receive them. They are like IOUs. Some day you may want to draw on them.

9. Make sure to follow up. This is the key to successful networking. It is easier to have the secretary put you through to the president if you have just had lunch with him or her.

10. Send "fuzzies." Every so often (one to three months), go through your contact file. If you haven't spoken to someone in a while, call to say hello or send a relevant article or note.

11. Remove unproductive and unethical contacts from your file: people who consistently break their agreements with you or the contacts you've given them, or people whose behavior does not coincide with their words.

Chapter 3 Summary

1. Follow the six guidelines for finding the right job.

2. Prepare yourself mentally and physically for the job search.

3. "Interview" your prospective bosses.

4. Find and work with the "right" networks and support groups.

5. Build your own MasterMind group.

getting started on the job

CONGRATULATIONS! You've got your first sales job. So what's next? A lot!

In 1976, I got my first real professional sales job with a "small" company called Xerox!

After going through several interviews, I was finally hired and told to report to the branch manager first thing on Monday morning the following week. I was so excited that I took my wife to a very expensive restaurant to celebrate the momentous occasion. It was a double win for me. Not only did I get the job in sales with a major corporation, but it also vindicated my being rejected by IBM the year before. Although the company would never admit it, it was mainly due to the fact that I was forty-five pounds overweight and had a beard.

I showed up at the Xerox branch office promptly at 8:30 a.m. that Monday morning, dressed in my blue blazer, gray pants, and new shoes. When I met the branch manager, I stood at attention, saluted, and said, "Mr. Mattia, Brian Azar reporting for duty!" He looked at me and said, "You must be the new recruit! Welcome to Xerox Corporation. Now go home, put on a three-piece gray suit, and report back this afternoon." IBMers wore blue suits; Xeroids wore gray. I didn't have a gray suit, so I had to go out and buy one. Fortunately, I was in New York City at the time and had a credit card, so I quickly went shopping and got the "right" suit, shirt, and tie. I had to pay a premium to get it altered the same day, but this job was worth it. When I got back to the branch, the branch manager looked at me and said, "That's much better. Now I need you to shave your beard and go on a diet." I said, "I'm not overweight. I'm just seven inches too short." He said, without cracking a smile, "No one at this branch is overweight."

I then told him that my beard covered scars from childhood and my wife would be upset if I had to remove it. He said, "None of my salespeople have a beard."

Given that I had just taken a job in a territory in which three people had quit or been fired in the past six months, with a quota that never did more than 15 percent of budget in the last year (one month it did 30 percent, but that was because Xerox double billed an account by mistake), I negotiated an agreed-on deal with the branch manager. Back in the 1970s, salespeople usually started off with a small salary and a nonaccountable guarantee for the first year. Then, they were on salary plus commission. Xerox salespeople also had to wait three to six months before they went to Xerox University in Leesburg, Virginia, for a two-week sales training program. I told my branch manager to cancel my guarantee and get me into the next open sales training class, and when I came back, the first month I missed 100 percent of quota, I'd shave off my beard. The second month, I'd go on a diet. He laughed so hard, he nearly fell off his chair, but he agreed to my terms. He figured he had nothing to lose. Neither did I.

The first day after my completed training, I started out at 7:30 a.m. in my territory. I went to a local corporate park that housed several small businesses. I had a brown bag with several fresh pastries and cookies. I waited for an owner to show up, and when the first one appeared, I introduced myself as the new Xerox salesperson and said I was there to "interview" him about his business. I told him that if he would put up the coffee, I'd provide the pastries. I then got "invited" in. I did the exact same thing with the secretaries and receptionists, except this time, I interviewed them about their bosses.

At the end of the first month, I hit 102 percent of quota and got to keep my beard. At the end of the second month, I hit 112 percent of quota. In fact, after three consecutive high production months, I started being awarded Salesman of the Month of the branch and became Rookie of the Year. The following year, I was the number two salesman in the country, achieving the prestigious President's Club award.

I then had to go to the Rochester, New York, Xerox headquarters to receive my award. My branch manager told me once again to shave my beard and lose some weight. Once again, I declined. This time, he told me to take a vacation before I went to receive my award. He then sent a Western Union telegram to the president of the company, explaining that when I showed up for the award, if I had a beard, a tan, and looked a bit heavy, it was because I was coming directly from my vacation! Six weeks later, the branch manager finally got rid of me. He recommended me for a sales manager's position at another branch. I took it.

My experiences as a sales manager will be left for another book, but the lessons learned, both as a new salesperson and a sales manager who had to hire six new salespeople quickly, gave me some additional insights and resources for this chapter.

As Yogi Berra allegedly once said, "You've got to be very careful if you don't know where you are going, because you may not get there." So let's start with your first sixty days on the job. First, forget about the Golden Rule in your workplace. The worst mistake you can make is to treat people the way you want to be treated. Instead, watch, listen, and learn how people want to be treated . . . their way. In business these days, there is a very short honeymoon, if any. You need to learn to keep your eyes and ears open and your mouth shut about 80 percent of the time. When you do open your mouth, make sure that it is mostly to ask questions and learn from the answers given. You also have to use your intuition and common sense, and to learn the corporate culture, language, and communication styles of the key players.

Most companies today have what they loosely call a ninety-day probationary period for new salespeople. This time frame gives them the opportunity to decide if and how you fit in, as well as how well you perform under different circumstances and situations.

For the first thirty days, get to know who the top salespeople are in your company and why they are successful. Approach each of them and invite them out to an early breakfast or lunch, your treat.

During these engagements, *do not* "kiss up" or "suck up" to these people; rather, acknowledge them for their success, interview them about how they got their position, and ask what they did, specifically, to learn the rules and politics of the organization. Ask them what they did to succeed their first ninety days on the job and what pitfalls to be on the look out for.

Find out from them what it is that they want or need and how you might help them, even if it's just to do some research. Ask them about their strategies for success, their goals, and their daily planning activities. Find out who their role models are or were when they first started. Learn their particular communication styles and preferences and begin to "model" them. (See Chapter 7, Establishing Rapport, for more details.)

Remember—your initial purpose is to connect with these people and begin to lay the groundwork for future, mutually beneficial, win–win relationships. Take the same approach and steps with your internal customer service and sales support teams. They have a wealth of knowledge and experience they can share, if someone would just listen to them and take notes. If your company has technical support, or consultants, who go out onto client sites, interview them too. They have creditability and leverage with the client and can help you with valuable insights, as well as possible referrals and introductions. Make sure you meet with your sales manager early on to get clearly defined roles, goals, objectives, and a fairly detailed job description, including all the possible reasons or conditions for termination. Yes, I said termination. It is much better and safer to know the ground rules for failure—as well as success—as early in the game as possible. Keep a running list of questions to cover with your sales manager, to be discussed no later than thirty days into the job. This is an excellent way to avoid "mutual mystification." It shows that you are willing to take the initiative and learn from your manager those things you're not clear about, as well as the willingness to ask early on: "How am I doing? What can I do better or differently?"

One of the most valuable tools you will have during your first ninety days, as well as your first year, will be your personal "playbook." In this playbook you will document specifically all the successes, failures, mistakes, and lessons you're learning during your first three months, so that you will know what to keep and enhance, reduce or eliminate, do differently, or change, in your action planning for the next ninety days, as well as the rest of the year. This playbook can also be used to document in detail your specific accomplishments within your territory—how you obtained new clients and tracked your prospects. It will also list the obstacles and hurdles that you may have encountered and overcame, along with the personal goals, objectives, and quotas you established as guidelines for yourself. This playbook will be the basis for your ninety-day review with your sales manager. If your manager hasn't scheduled one, then ask for one so that you both can check on and review your progress and jointly chart your growth for the rest of the year.

During your first year in sales, do some research on your company's beginnings, its founders, and the industry in general. Get as much information as you possibly can on the competitive players, both big and small. Find out which companies have "great" reputations for quality, service, and reliability.

Discover who their top salespeople are and where they hang out, places such as chambers of commerce, industry trade shows, workshops, and conferences. When you meet them, introduce yourself and acknowledge them accordingly. You never know when a situation may arise when you might actually refer some business to them in the future, business that you or your company cannot perform for a client or prospect, but that they can. Remember the rule: "What goes around comes around." The best salespeople do what is in their clients' best interest, and that might include an introduction to another company that may have an excellent product or service that you don't currently provide.

On the other side of the coin, find out as quickly as possible which are the worst companies and salespeople in your industry and marketplace and stay far away.

A final note on "dressing for success." In the movie *All That Jazz*, Bob Fosse wakes up every morning, takes his shower, pops his pills, looks in the mirror, and says, "It's showtime!" He then puts on his "costume" for the day. What you put on to go to work in the office or out in the field is your costume for that day. Choose wisely and, accordingly, you'll be more successful!

Notice the dress style of senior management, especially your immediate boss, in your office and dress to their level. Have an extra shirt and tie in the office as a back up, in case of an emergency or accident, or an extra blouse and hosiery, if you are a woman. When you're out in your territory, you dress to the style of your prospects and clients, even if, once in a while, you have to take off your tie— or other accessory, if you are a woman. This concept of dressing up or down to the level of your colleagues, staff, and client base is called matching and mirroring, and is discussed further in Chapter 7.

In conclusion to this chapter, here is some final counsel for you, to be noted and applied during your first day, week, month, and year in your new sales position:

1. Eighty per cent of your success will come from the positive attitude, actions, and behavior that you exhibit during your first year in sales.

2. It's not what happens to you in the first year that counts; it is how you respond to, learn from, and adjust to what happens—the appropriateness of the actions you take.

Chapter 4 Summary

1. Interview the top salespeople to discover their mindsets, strategies, and actions regarding success.

2. Look and listen attentively 80 percent of the time and ask qualifying questions 10 per cent of the time. Use what's left for speaking.

3. Create a "playbook" for your first year in sales and use it daily.

4. Dress to the level of senior management in your office and of your client base when in the field.

5

say goodbye to the old game of sales

The traditional self-focused selling approach is no longer effective because today's new buyers are unwilling to follow you. They don't want to be "sold." They want to make educated buying decisions. To make a sale, you must join them on their buying path.

–Kevin Davis, *Getting Into Your Customer's Head*

OVER THE YEARS, I have observed the mistakes of many pushy, pressure-oriented salespeople. Although their actual approaches may vary, there are many common pitfalls that trap them. Among the most common are:

1. They talk instead of listening, otherwise known as "blabbermouth syndrome." Blabbermouths don't sell; they merely annoy people into handing over their money. They assume that if they can fill in every second of silence with useless (or even useful) chatter about how great their products are, then every objection in the prospect's mind will magically disappear. This isn't selling. It's merely irritating the prospect.

Any time a salesperson is talking, the client is formulating objections. That's just the way the human mind works. Anytime a salesperson is listening, the client is probably still formulating objections . . . but at least the salesperson will have an idea about what those objections might be.

2. They pitch their products or services instead of asking questions. Salespeople love spouting out solutions to problems. In fact, most companies are no longer in the business of selling products. Instead, they are now in the business of providing solutions. The only thing wrong with this is that too many sales professionals attempt to tell the prospect the solution before they even understand the problem. If salespeople were held accountable for their solutions, as doctors are for their prescriptions, they would be forced to examine the problem thoroughly before proposing a cure—at the risk of malpractice! The salesperson must ask questions up front to ensure a complete understanding of the prospect's perspective.

3. They answer unasked questions. When a prospect makes a statement such as, "Your price is too high," most sales professionals automatically switch into a defensive mode. Often they begin a lengthy speech on quality or value, or they might respond with a concession or a price reduction. If prospects can get a discount by merely making a statement, then maybe they shouldn't buy yet—until they try something more powerful to get an even better price. "Your price is too high" is not a question. And it does not require an answer.

4. They fail to get the prospect to reveal a budget up front. How can the salesperson possibly propose a solution without knowing the prospect's priorities regarding a problem? Knowing whether there is money allocated for a project will help the salesperson distinguish between the prospect who is committed to solving a problem or the one who is merely committed to "talking about" solving the problem. The amount of money the prospect sees investing to solve a problem helps determine whether a solution is feasible, and if so, what approach matches the prospect's ability to pay.

5. They make too many follow-up calls when the sale is actually dead. Whether it is a stubborn attitude to turn every prospect into a customer or ignorance of the fact that the sale is truly dead, too much time is spent chasing accounts that don't qualify for a product or service. This should have been detected far earlier in the sales interview process (more about that later).

6. They fail to get a commitment to purchase *before* making a presentation. Salespeople are too willing to jump at the opportunity to show how smart they are by making features and benefit presentations about their products. They miss their true goal to make a sale and end up merely educating their prospects, who then have all the information they need to help buy from a competitor.

7. They chat about everything and avoid starting the interview process. Building rapport is necessary and desirable, but all too often small talk doesn't end, and the interview process doesn't actually begin. Unfortunately, the prospect usually recognizes this before the sales professional. The result is that the salesperson is back on the street wondering how he or she did with the prospect.

8. They would rather hear "I want to think it over" than "No." Prospects are constantly ending the sales interview with the standard "think it over" line. The salesperson accepts this indecision and even sympathizes with the prospect. It's easier for salespeople to tell their sales managers that their prospects may buy in the future than to say that a prospect is not a qualified candidate for the product. After all, wasn't it the salesperson's job to go out and get prospects to say yes? Getting the prospect to say no can also produce feelings of personal rejection or failure.

9. They see themselves as beggars instead of doctors. Salespeople don't view their time with a prospect as time spent conducting an interview to find out if the prospect qualifies to do business with their company. All too often, a prospect remains a suspect and never gets to the more qualified level of prospect. Salespeople often find themselves hoping, wishing, and even begging for the opportunity to "just show my wares" and maybe make a sale. This is unlike the physician, who examines the patient thoroughly before making a recommendation. A doctor uses questions as instruments to conduct a qualifying examination of the prospect.

10. They work without a systematic approach to selling. Salespeople often find themselves ad-libbing or using a hit-or-miss approach to making the sale. They allow the prospect to control the process. Salespeople often leave the sales call feeling confused and not knowing where they stand. This happens because they don't know where they have been and what the next step should be. The importance of following a specific sequence and controlling the steps through the process is vital to the organized sales professional's success.

Do you make any of these mistakes yourself?

A Self-Evaluation Exercise: Feeling the Pressure

Here's a quick exercise. Imagine this scenario: It's the last week of the month and you haven't made even half your quota. Your boss seems increasingly annoyed with your performance and there are three other "hungry" reps eager to move in on your territory. Obviously, you're a little nervous because your job is on the line and you desperately need to make three sales before the day's end. So here it is: 10:30 a.m. and you've just approached the office of your first prospect . . . . You step out of your vehicle . . . . You take your first steps toward the door . . .

Now take a look at a list of the typical things most salespeople think about before walking through that door and approaching a prospect:

1. "Gee whiz. I hope I make this sale . . ."

2. "God, I really need this sale . . ."

3. "Please, God! Just make 'em say yes."

4. "This prospect better not turn out like all the rest . . ."

5. "All I need is the smallest hook of interest and I know I can close this deal."

6. "If only I had some good quality leads—prospects actually interested in what I'm offering . . ."

7. "Where should I go to eat today?"

8. "I hope I smell all right . . ."

9. "Do I have something in my teeth?"

Or a salesperson into motivational psychology might be thinking:

1. "I can do it! I can do it! Yes! By golly, I can do it!"

2. "I like myself . . . I like myself . . . I like myself!"

3. "I'm the sales king of the universe!"

4. "Grrrrrrr! Watch out prospect: The sales lion is here!"

Where is the so-called sales pressure as you approach the door? On you? On your prospect?

Obviously, the pressure is all on you—and that's before you even knock on the door! Think about the implications of this approach and how it affects your prospect, and then ask yourself this question: *How would I feel about selling if there were never any pressure at all?*

Before reading the next section, make a list of ten reasons why selling without the slightest hint of pressure would be more beneficial to both you and your prospect.

The New World of Pressure-Free Selling

In Aesop's fable "The Wind and the Sun," the two argue over who is stronger.

> Seeing a traveler walking down the road, they decided to settle the issue by trying to make the traveler take off his coat. The wind went first, but the harder the wind blew, the more closely the traveler wrapped his coat

around him. Then the sun came out and began to shine. Soon the traveler felt the sun's warmth and took off his coat. The sun had won.[1]

The mindset of an "old school" sales approach is a lot like the cold wind trying to blow open the clenched arms of a prospect. And despite what you may think or believe, today's prospects do have clenched arms against whatever a salesperson says or does, whether we want them to or not. But it doesn't have to be this way.

PRESCRIPTION FOR SUCCESS

When what you're doing isn't working, do anything different. When what you're doing is working, do anything different.

The Old Game of Pressure-Selling: Another Simple Exercise

Emotions and attitudes are very powerful and ultimately impact how we handle, or mishandle, sales situations. When you experience anger, fear, anxiety, hostility, pride, selfishness, overenthusiasm, distrust, and a slew of other feelings, you set yourself up for disaster.

In this exercise, you look at some commonly made selling mistakes, and more important, you look closely at the emotions and feelings that surround them.

PART 1. On a piece of paper folded in half, write these situations on one side of the sheet:

1. Talking instead of listening

2. Assuming rather than questioning

3. Failing to fully identify the prospects problems, needs, budget, etc.

4. Giving up quickly

5. Preferring a prospect to say "I'll think about it" rather than "no"

6. Not answering the "what's in it for me" question from your prospect

7. Dodging new prospects

8. Failing to get adequate training, coaching, or support

9. Working with a plan

10. Allowing fear to be your guide

Next, go back up to item number 1 and start to list the emotions, feelings, and circumstances that lead up to these types of mistakes. For example, for item number 1 you might write something like:

1. Talking instead of listening—emotions experienced:

    a. Impatience

    b. Frustration

    c. Desperation

    d. Fear

Continue down the sheet until you have done this for each item.

Note: When you look at all of the emotions these pressure-oriented actions conjure up, you may feel a bit overwhelmed. That's good. You want to associate a lot of pain with these old school methods and notions—and mistakes—of selling. That way, when stressful situations arise, as they always do, you won't feel so compelled to fall back on familiar, ineffective habits.

PART 2. Now that you've blown the dust off of those uncomfortable emotions and feelings, let's delve a little deeper into each of the situations. Beginning with the first situation, talking instead of listening, spend some quiet time contemplating—and recording in your notebook—the *negative effects* of not listening. In fact, for each of these situations, I recommend writing an ongoing, stream-of-consciousness, five-to-seven-minute monologue. Here are some primers to get you started:

- ✗ Ask yourself a question like: *What's it like to really listen?* or *What's it like when someone's really listening to me?* For a lot of people, the answer might start something like this: For the most part, if I'm really honest with myself, I know that I don't really listen to anyone—or anything—at all.

- ✗ You can listen for what's around you right now. How many things can you hear that you didn't notice until this moment, when you began to consciously focus on listening?

- ✗ Or you can contemplate things from another perspective: Have any of my friends or family members ever complained that I'm a terrible listener? If so, why? If not, why? Perhaps they're just being polite.

We're all terrible listeners, every one of us. We don't like to listen to anyone at all—unless, of course, they're talking about us. Think about it: When you look at a picture of you with all your friends, whose face do you notice first? Have you ever looked closely at a picture in which everyone but you looks obviously bad and thought: "Boy, that's a really good picture."

We love when others listen to us, but we hate to listen to others. We love even the dullest conversation about ourselves and resist even the most fascinating conversation that pertains to other people. It's true. How many times have you interjected a dull anecdote into another person's otherwise interesting story?

Note: So now, when your colleagues, friends, or spouse ask you what you learned today, you can say: "I learned that I never really listen." Don't be surprised if you don't get much disagreement.

Why It's Important to Associate a Lot of Pain with Old Ways of Selling

It may seem a bit morbid to harp on the negative side of selling, but over time you'll associate more pain and frustration with the "old ways" and more pleasurable, happy feelings with the new game of pressure-free selling.

In fact, as you think about your role as a traditional, old school salesperson, you should consider:

1. Most people you meet will not want to talk to you.

2. Most people you meet will not like you.

3. Most people you meet will think you're lying to them.

4. Most people you meet will then lie to you. ("Oh, you've caught me at a bad time. My child has just coughed up his dinner on the living room floor . . . Could you come back in another three years?")

5. Most people you meet will be annoyed, agitated, and visibly upset.

And from *your* side, let's not forget:

1. You'll get burned out in a matter of months.

2. Your friends, loved ones, and family members will start plotting against you. After all, how can you use all these shady tactics on your customers and not expect them to rub off on everyone else in your life?

"But is it really all that bad?" you might ask.

My answer: "Of course not." In fact, did you know there is an upside to the "old" game of selling?

Yep, there is, and the *biggest* upside of traditional selling is that it actually works! Provided, of course, that your prospect is one of the following:

1. Very stupid

2. Too exhausted to fight back

3. Too drunk to care either way

4. A recent recipient of electro-shock therapy

5. Brain dead

I'd like you to stretch your imagination for a moment. I'd like you to consider a world in which . . .

1. Selling becomes fun!

2. Selling becomes profitable; people actually enjoy doing business with you.

3. Selling becomes simple and natural; you don't have to act one way with your customers and another way with your family and friends.

4. Selling becomes something you can do all the time, avoiding the "schizophrenia" of ordinary selling professionals.

5. Selling becomes immensely interesting.

Sound far-fetched? I've reeducated thousands of salespeople to see their profession in exactly this light. They not only learn to enjoy the process of selling, but they make more money, create more opportunities, and have more fun than they ever thought possible.

But It Does Take Some Work

Unfortunately, nothing worthwhile comes easy. The new game of pressure-free selling does require work, lots and lots of it. But think about it: Becoming a famous musician takes more than getting on MTV and singing a few songs. There are usually years and years of preparation, practice, and sacrifice before a performer ever steps on a stage. And as a world-class salesperson, you need to put in lots of hours refining your skills.

But (and this is a *big* "but") the harder you work selling this way, the more *charismatic, fascinating,* and *magnetic* you become. Everyone you know suddenly wants to be around you more. It's an inevitable reciprocal law: You get what you give out. Give out garbage (the old game of sales is always selling garbage) and that's all you'll get back.

So there it is: Both games require preparation *and* hard work.

What you need to ask yourself, over and over and over again, is this: What in the world am I specifically preparing for? In other words, what do you really want out of your life and work?

AN EXERCISE IN SELF-KNOWLEDGE: WHY SUCCESS?

List six or seven reasons why you want to become successful in sales. Use the following questions to stimulate your thinking:

What's really driving you?

Is it the money? (Be honest.)

Do you like (or not like) people? (Be extremely honest.)

Do you like the freedom working for yourself?

Take a few minutes to complete this assignment now.

The 60-Second Infomercial Exercise: Who's Number 1?

This is the last, but most important, exercise before we get into the nuts and bolts tactics. It's a simple exercise, but quite profound, so please approach it seriously.

Scenario: Your very rich aunt just died, and instead of leaving you her fortune, she left you a sixty-second commercial spot for this year's Super Bowl game. The only catch: You have to sell *yourself* in those sixty seconds.

You're about to stand before close to a billion people and sell yourself for one full minute. This amounts to about 120 words—approximately one double-spaced page of typewritten copy. What will you say?

Remember: Honesty and sincerity are the keys to your selling success.

Remember also: Extra points will be given for the most creative presentation.

After you've finished the assignment, move on to the next section for a three-minute evaluation of your infomercial.

YOUR THREE-MINUTE EVALUATION

Step 1: Take out your written infomercial and a pen.

Step 2: Read over your script and circle the pronouns I, me, and my.

Question 1: How many circles are on your page?

Question 2: How much relevance do you think each of those circles has to your audience?

Tip: Hold your sheet up to the light. For every circle you see, imagine a bullet hole through your presentation . . . because that's exactly what it is.

Introducing the 10-Step Sales Interview™ Approach

The old adage holds true: The more you think about yourself, the less others think of you. In the 10-Step Sales Interview that follows in Part 2 of this book, you learn a simple, step-by-step blueprint for pressure-free, other-oriented selling.

You become more like a doctor, caring for and administering to your patients, than a hustler, caring only for yourself. In sales, we often find ourselves trapped in old ways of thinking because it's easier to just go with the flow, but if we're not careful, that flow could take us someplace we may not want to go. Following along with the strategies outlined in this book, however, you not only become happier, more relaxed, and infinitely more fulfilled, but you also profit from your career like never before.

You don't have to get sick to get better. In a famous study, laboratory rats learned to run a maze differently when their prize was moved. Human beings usually have trouble letting go and trying something new. If you keep on doing the same things and getting the same results, and those aren't the results you're looking for, it's time to change. Why not do something about it now?

Chapter 5 Summary

With traditional, "old school" selling:

1. Most people you meet will not want to talk to you.

2. Most people you meet will not like you.

3. Most people you meet will think you're lying to them.

4. Most people you meet will then lie to you ("Oh, you've caught me at a bad time. My child has just coughed up his dinner on the living room floor . . . . Could you come back in another three years?")

5. Most people you meet will be annoyed, agitated, and visibly upset.

So let's not forget the possible consequences for you:

You'll get burned out in a matter of months. Your friends, loved ones, and family members will start plotting against you, because how can you use all these shady tactics on your customers and not expect them to rub off on everyone else in your life?

---

[1] Taken from *The Fall of Advertising and the Rise of PR*, by Al Ries and Laura Ries, New York: HarperBusiness, 2002.

PART TWO

Getting There

The 10-Step Interview
for Sales Success

10	The After Sale
9	Close
8	Reinforcement
7	Presentation
6	Review

If qualified, continue to number 6. If not qualified, terminate the process.

5	Decision Maker
4	Budget
3	Finding the Pain
2	Rapport
1	Pre-Call Planning

step 1: **pre-call planning**

THE DICTIONARY defines the word *prospect* as "a potential buyer or customer; a likely candidate." Thus, prospecting can be simply defined as the act of identifying those potential customers who are most likely to purchase your product or service. In fact, all sales situations can be viewed as *the seller looking for a buyer.*

In order to maximize their earning potential, sales professionals must continuously develop new customers. The techniques of prospecting are second in importance only to the sales presentation itself. But regardless of how dynamic or convincing your sales skills are, you must first find the prospect in order to display those sales skills. There are numerous prospecting techniques.

Being Creative

Each prospecting technique can be a valuable sales tool. Certainly choose those that work for you; however, successful sales professionals are usually those who use a wide variety of techniques.

It's also important to develop techniques that apply to your specific areas. For example, when you frequently come across a particular stall or objection, learn to deal with it up front. Salespeople who have a high-priced product or service can deal with price objections before the client does by saying, "Mr. or Ms. Prospect, I appreciate your interest in my product (or service), but before we get too far, I must tell you that we are never the low bidder. Is this going to be a problem?"

Dealing with stalls and objections up front tends to neutralize them—and it takes the pressure off the salesperson.

Meeting the Prospect

Before meeting your prospects, your concern should be who and where these potential customers are. How do you go about finding new prospects? There are a number of sources that can aid you in discovering this important information. The initial information you want to know from these various sources are:

Company or individual name/address

Telephone number

Company officers (president, CEO, etc.) and number of employees

Type of business or product line

Main and branch offices

This basic information assists you in understanding the prospect's business situation. Now you know something about the prospect. This data can aid you in your "sales interview."

For example, if you sell copiers and are considering approaching a business that has 250 employees, you can be certain that it has a wide variety of copying needs. Knowing a prospect's circumstances also increases the confidence a prospect has in *you*, for you have taken the time to find out about the prospect's situation. That shows concern.

Sources for Generating Leads

Dun and Bradstreet: Million Dollar Directory
Lists approximately 39,000 U.S. companies with a worth of $1,000,000 or more.

Standard & Poor's Register
Alphabetical listing of more than 36,000 U.S. and Canadian companies; volume 1 gives addresses, telephone numbers, company officers, etc.

Chamber of Commerce Publications
Most cities have an active chamber of commerce. Contact them for lists of companies in specific industries that are doing business in your area.

Thomas Register of American Manufacturers
A comprehensive listing of American manufacturing firms; volume 7 is the alphabetical listing giving the address, telephone number, branch offices, product line, subsidiaries, and principal officers.

State Industrial Directories
These give information for each manufacturer in a particular state. The data given includes address, phone number, company officers, and number of employees.

Professional/Trade Association Directories
Doctors, lawyers, accountants, engineers, purchasing agents, and most other professionals have organizations or associations that include a listing of all of their members. The membership is usually on a yearly basis, thus the listing is up to date.

Newspapers/Trade Periodicals

These are an often-overlooked source of business leads—especially newspapers. In the business and public notice sections of most newspapers, you can find a lot of valuable information. For example, *Crain's New York Business* publishes a list of the top companies several times each year, with their addresses, phone numbers, CEOs, and other useful information. These lists are organized into such leading-edge topics of interest as "The 500 Fastest Growing Companies in the U.S."

Internet

Virtually all of these sources and thousands more can easily be found by doing a simple search on the Internet. This creates more possibilities than ever in the history of modern business. It is amazing what you can discover and learn by going to a company's Web site—from information on its key management to its products and services, and even its successes. Make sure you visit the media and press release sections. This is where you will find recent activities and "wins."

Rules of the Road in Telephoning

If you're making your first contact by telephone, there are a few basics you need to keep in mind that will ensure more effective calls.

1. *Attitude.* Establish a productive, motivated, confident state within yourself that is free of fears, which you can trigger every time you pick up the phone. Relax and take a few deep breaths.

2. *Preparation.* Have your lead sheets before you, organized in the order you plan to make your calls. Make sure pencils, pens, paper, and forms are at hand. Know your purpose for the call and what you are going to say before you dial the phone. Have a 5-by-7-inch mirror to watch yourself so you don't take yourself too seriously when you call. If you want

to increase your telephone sales, try standing up and walking around. Your passion will come across much better!

3. *Ask for Help.* Each time you contact someone initially, ask for help, such as spellings or pronunciation of people's names or useful information about the company.

4. *Repeat the Prospect's First Name.* When you begin your conversation, make sure you ask for and then get permission to use the contact's first name. Then, each time you mention the prospect's name, the person will pay close attention to the next five words you say.

5. *Listen Actively.* People who earn a living contacting others are often the world's worst listeners. Sit up and listen! Many important buying signals are lost because we talk when we should listen.

6. *Mirror Your Prospect.* Enter your prospect's world by matching vocabulary, rate of speech, phrase construction, volume, and mood (more about all of these in Chapter 7). People who tend to sound like each other are more likely to like each other.

7. *Ask Qualifying Questions.* Your job on the phone is to separate prospects from suspects before making lengthy presentations. A "qualified" prospect is one who has a need, budget, a timeline for action, and is the one who can say yes, as opposed to the ones who can only say no.

8. *Use Strategic Pauses.* When you ask a question or make a comment that is intended to get the prospect to respond, pause. Ask the question and wait—at least six seconds—for the answer.

9. *Get Specific Commitments (Up-Front Contracts).* Always know what is to happen next. Make sure there is no "mutual mystification," confusion, or misunderstanding by either or both

parties as to what clearly has been said and/or agreed to, including the next steps or actions to be taken.

10. *Read Your Own Publications.* Make certain you receive and read everything that is printed about your product, service, market niche, and industry.

11. *Keep a Prospect (Contact) File.* For each prospect contacted, keep notes on follow-up, pertinent business data, and personal comments that can be used in future conversations.

It would make sense to record the communication style and particular likes or preferences of your prospect for future follow-up, using the "fuzzy file" approach to continue to establish rapport.

Setting the Mood

Look around your work space. Is it a pleasant place to be? If not, do what you can to make it more livable. Get some plants or pictures. Make sure there is at least something nearby that you like to look at. Get a cordless telephone; this allows you to get up from the desk and walk around. If possible, get a headset. Freedom of movement allows you to feel, and therefore sound, more natural and relaxed.

Start by memorizing the script you intend to use. Once you have the basic script down, you are free to ad lib with confidence—with something to fall back on if you get into trouble. Memorization is also necessary so that you sound more natural on the phone. Very few people can read and not sound like they're reading a paragraph out of, say, *Ivanhoe.*

There have been some proven rapport-building phrases and techniques incorporated into the scripts provided for you in this book. Use them and add to them as time allows. It is vital that you spend time in the first few seconds on this important step. The success of the rest of the call may depend on it.

You Can't "Sell" Anything

The key to many parts of the scripts that follow is that you are not meant to look, sound, or act like the average salesperson. Remember: The purpose of your research is not to *sell* anything. It is simply to:

1. Gather information

2. Qualify prospects, while elegantly rejecting the ones that don't qualify

3. Set up interviews with those who do

In all cases, remember to ask for a referral! And please, relax. Enjoy. Breathe deeply. Don't take rejection personally, and have some fun.

PREPARE IN ADVANCE TO SIDESTEP PUT-OFFS

At various stages in the direct selling process, you may have run into some common objections or stalling tactics. Here are some suggestions on how to handle them.

Prospect: Send me literature.

You: I'd love to do that, but I wouldn't know what to send you. It will only take me about ten minutes to find out more specifically what information you might need, and then I will be able to provide you with everything. Do you have the time to talk now, or can you set a time for me to call you?

Or,

You: Can you help me? What specifically are you hoping the literature will show or tell you to enable you to make an appointment to talk with me? *Then deal with that, specifically, on the phone.*

Among the other objections you might encounter are:

1. **Prospect:** No time. We're just too busy. We won't commit [for whatever reason].

You: Can I ask you a personal question, off the record? Are the [events, machines, people, whatever your product or service] important to you, important enough to invest fifteen minutes of your time and my expertise? Great! Get out your calendar.

2. **Prospect:** We have a current supplier.

You: I'd be concerned if you didn't have one. The reason I say that is because most of our clients currently have, or have had in the past, at least one other supplier. Can I ask you a question? Does that mean you're closed to talking with someone who might be able to help you or your organization?

3. **Prospect:** We're happy with our current suppliers.

You: Great! And does that mean that they never make a mistake or nothing ever goes wrong?

Or,

You: Does that mean your mind is closed to talking with someone new, who may have something to help you and your organization save money, save time, and improve [whatever area is in question]?

Sometimes, you may reach a definitive no. Remember, that's not so bad. At least you know where you stand, and you can devote your energies to more promising prospects. You can even turn a negative into a positive. Here's how.

Prospect: No. Absolutely not!

You: Gee, it doesn't look like I can help you. Maybe you can help me. Do you know anyone who might be in need of my expertise and knowledge or might need our product or service?

PRESCRIPTION FOR SUCCESS

Always ask for a referral. In this way, you can make every call pay off.

Part 1: The First Interview

"MAY I CALL YOU JOHN?"

It is important always to ask permission to use a person's first name. This helps build rapport in two different ways:

1. It shows respect.

2. When you ask for permission to do something and they say yes, it endears you to them.

People generally appreciate being allowed to do something for you in much the same way that a host or hostess appreciates being allowed to get you something to drink. It puts them at ease and they feel better. This is a very subtle, yet powerful rapport-building tool.

Once they do give you permission, don't forget to use their name once in a while. Don't overdo it, or you will sound like a salesperson. However, studies show that people do tune into the first few words that are said after they hear their name. This can be very useful in adding emphasis to what you are saying.

If they say no, you must respect that. Not all people wish to be called by their first name, and by asking, rather that assuming, you may do more to build rapport than you could have done in any other way. Respond, "Certainly Mr. Smith, but if at some point that changes, please let me know."

"IS THIS A GOOD TIME TO TALK?"

Always remember to ask the prospects if this is a good time to talk. It makes them stop what they are doing for a moment and listen to what you are going to say. It shows them that you think what you are going to say is important, and it demonstrates respect for the other person's time, acknowledging your intrusion. If they say it is not a good time, tell them you understand, and ask when would be a good time for you to call back. This simple question can avoid the problem of getting to the point of your call only to find that they have to go. When you do call back, it is no longer research. You can honestly say, "Mr. Smith asked me to call at 3:00." The objective is to always maintain control, and this subtly helps a sales professional do just that.

THE COLUMBO APPROACH

Remember to ask for help. One of the basic premises of this selling system is that people make themselves feel better by finding someone else who is not so well off as they are. This is sad but true. Learning to use phrases like, "Can you help me?" and "I'm not sure," is a subtle way to get your prospects to drop their defenses and open up. The "Columbo Approach" to professional selling has been proven much more effective than the "know-it-all" approach. Try it out and see how well it works for you.

PRESCRIPTION FOR SUCCESS

The "Columbo Approach" to professional selling has been proven much more effective than the James Bond "Know-It-All" approach.

As a side note, playing a role in the sales cycle by telling the secretary or prospect that you need help also serves to remove yourself from the sale. In this way, you can relax and not take things so personally.

WHEN YOU GET TO YOUR PROSPECT'S OFFICE

When you get to the prospect's office, don't sit down in the lobby. Stand, walk around, breathe deeply, and notice anything you can about the company. Pay attention to what the lobby tells you about the image the company is trying to portray. If they spent a lot of money decorating the lobby, chances are that "we don't have any money" is a stall, and you know it is not really true. Read the brochures that are left out for the public. Think about what they are telling you and the public. Make sure you read any plaques or framed announcements that may be on the wall.

And again, whatever you do, don't sit down! The physiological act of sitting puts you in a different state. It's more kinesthetic and therefore a more vulnerable position to be in mentally. Your fears and uncertainties are more liable to surface when you are sunk deep into a comfortable sofa. Sitting can also make for an awkward first moment with your prospects as you try to get up, shake their hand, and pick up whatever you may be carrying, all at the same time. Women, especially, can find this an awkward moment. By standing, you avoid all of this and put yourself on an equal level with your prospects from the get-go. Tell the receptionist, "No thank you, I've been sitting all day." And if it's first thing in the morning, you may add, "I start early."

As you are being taken to the prospect's office or meeting place, pay attention to the other people you see and their surroundings. Are the people happy or are they anxious? Do the work areas look organized? Is the place clean? Is it crowded? Do they have state-of-the-art office machines? How large is the company? This type of information can give you a great deal of insight into a company's priorities and decision-making strategies. Take advantage of this "inside look" and the opportunity it creates.

One final suggestion in terms of pre-call planning: For those who are courageous, practice this strategy on your first interviews with very small, inconsequential "suspects" for a while until you feel comfortable.

Go in naked, so to speak; that is, don't bring anything—no briefcase, no brochures, no presentation materials at all. Not even pen or paper! Just bring your business card in your pocket. If you have things you need to have with you, leave the briefcase or bag with the receptionist or in the reception room closet.

By doing this, you take away a lot of the fear from the prospect, who might be wary of the "heavy sell." When you have nothing with you, it shows them that you must be there to do only one thing: talk. This relaxes the prospects and makes them more open. I'll go into this more as I get into the later steps.

Remember, you are still in the information gathering stage, not the presentation stage (see Chapter 12), so you do not need to show them anything until they qualify.

Just say that you customize all your work and that after the first interview, you will provide them with what they need.

Keep your word.

This is an information-gathering interview, not a dog and pony show.

Making the First Thirty Seconds Count

It is imperative to create a short, concise "commercial" for yourself, your company, your product, or your service. Done well, this also serves to draw the prospect in by highlighting problems that you solve or major benefits that you have to offer. This helps create a need for your product or service, something you must do anyway before a sale can be made.

This commercial is not the same as your sixty-second-infomercial exercise in the first chapter. Here, you want to convey, quickly and concisely, the bare-bones "essence" of what you have to offer your prospect. This is otherwise known as an "elevator speech."

Start your statement with, "We are in the business of . . . ." In time, you will find that many different commercials are necessary, depending on what industry and audience you are speaking to. There are also viral places in the phone scripts that call for your commercial, so create it now before you go on.

For social, informal, and formal networking events, you can use the following ten-step procedure, which is designed to help people who may not be getting the results they want at such events when they are asked, "What do you do?"

Face-to-Face Interviews

1. Have a firm handshake.

2. Make good eye contact.

3. Smile!

4. Repeat the person's name (and remember it).

5. Ask questions.

6. Tell them what you do (your commercial).

7. Ask them more questions regarding their use of your product or service.

8. Get their card.

9. Write on the back of it.

10. Follow up.

Using a blank sheet of paper, create a short paragraph that describes what you do via explaining the benefits of your product or service. In this way, people judge the value of your product or service in relation to what they perceive it can do for them now, not on what it might have done for them, or for others, in the past. For the first draft, talk about your product or service in universal terms. This is useful when addressing groups. After you have perfected this, you may wish to customize different versions to present to people in specific markets or industries. In time, you learn how to gather information in Step 5 that influences what you say in Step 6.

Making Your Commercial

The following questions should help you determine what benefits and solutions you want people to understand when they hear about your product or service. List the universal benefits of owning or using your product or service.

1. What problems are solved by owning or using your product or service?

2. What is your market?

3. What makes you, your product, or your service special or unique?

Now go back over Steps 1–4 to notice any patterns emerging. If, over time, something keeps coming up repeatedly, it may be worth highlighting. Ask yourself what things would sound particularly powerful or important to a prospective customer. Keeping these things in mind, write a brief paragraph that highlights why someone needs you, your product, or service. Start your paragraph with: "We are in the business of helping people/companies that may not be getting the results they want in the area of . . ."

A FEW EXAMPLES

Sales Training: We are in the business of helping individuals/ corporations who *may not be getting* the results they want or need in their prospecting, closing ratios, telemarketing, or revenue growth.

Life Insurance: We are in the business of helping people *who may not be getting* peace of mind, security, equity, and future financial freedom.

Commercial Real Estate: We are in the business of helping companies *who may not be getting* the benefits of current market conditions.

Residential Real Estate: We are in the business of helping individuals *who may not be getting* the results they want from the marketing, advertising, and servicing their current agents are providing.

Caterer: We are in the business of helping individuals and organizations *that may not be getting* that special personal touch that they want and need in the catering of their private parties or corporate affairs.

Freelance Illustrator: We're in the business of helping companies and individuals *who may not be getting* the image they want in their brochures, on their letterheads and business cards, and in their advertising, to be more in line with the image they have of themselves.

Computer Consultant: We are in the business of helping companies *who might not be getting* the results they want in terms of employee productivity, keeping track of information, and communication between departments.

Telecommunications/Data Transmission: We are in the business of helping individuals and organizations *who may not be getting* the rates, services, or reliability they need in a timely fashion from their current vendors or carriers.

Questions Are the Answer

Questioning is by far the most important skill to develop as a master sales professional. The processes of elegant questioning and gathering information are paramount to the Sales Doctor® philosophy. It is what sets you apart from the dreaded used-car-dealer stereotype. Pay particular attention to this section and practice the techniques outlined here. They will become an integral part of your selling script. The success of your entire sales track depends on effective questioning skills.

As the Sales Doctor, I have often maintained that your success in selling is directly proportional to the amount of information you don't give away for free. In other words, *telling* isn't *selling*. For you to stop selling and simply allow people to buy, you must ask them how they want to be sold. They will tell you. You just have to know how to listen—and how to ask the right questions. God gave you two ears and one mouth for a reason. On a sales call, you should be listening twice as much as you speak, and when speaking, you should be asking questions. Therefore, there are some simple rules of questioning you need to understand.

The Ten Rules of Questioning

1. Most prospects lie. If you ask the average person to describe salespeople, they will most likely use words like *loud, pushy, obnoxious, liars, insensitive,* and the like. It's no wonder. To the average person, a salesperson looks like a vulture waiting on a telephone pole for the chicken to cross the road so that he can swoop down and attack. The professional salesperson is often perceived as impolite and either impersonal or inappropriately friendly.

So, you see, most prospects think it's okay to lie to us because we lie to them. We taught them to lie: "He's in a meeting." "I'm too busy." "Send me literature." "I'll think about it." These are all defense mechanisms that prospects have developed against the loud, pushy, aggressive, stereotype of a salesperson. Don't hold it against them. Just understand it and deal with it.

2. Forget most of the things your mother told you. You don't want to have your mother with you during a sales call. Your mother had rules that applied when you were young that you may have to release now. Things like, "Don't talk to strangers," and "When I ask you a question, you answer me!" are examples of things to forget.

3. Put your ego aside. In order to be successful, we all need to be confident and prepared. Your prospects will sense it if you are not, and they will question your credibility. At times, it is important to ask for help in order to gather important information from your prospects. So don't be afraid to say things like, "I'm not sure," and "Can you help me?" These two questions can be used to gather information, defuse resistance, and build rapport.

4. Stop talking your way out of sales (and start questioning your way in.) As an educated sales professional, it's natural to want to demonstrate your knowledge to your prospect as much as possible. But stop! Stop giving it away. Stop talking and start asking. Get them to clarify exactly what it is they want to know.

It's your job to ask questions that zero in on their needs, problems, concerns, budget, and decision-making policies—before you get into your presentation. That means on the first call! Be prepared to say things like, "Gee, you're on page 12 and I'm still on page 1." Or, "I'm not sure you should use me. Can you help me?" and, "I need to get some more information before I can answer that."

5. When you're talking, you're not selling. Listen. Listen. Listen. This is the most vital part of questioning. Remember what you are trying to achieve. The whole purpose of questioning is to get your prospect to open up and talk, so bite your tongue if you have to, but keep your prospect talking. A question like, "Oh?" gives them no choice but to expound on what they have just said.

6. To put the shoe on the other foot, remember the "rule of three." Don't assume that you know why your prospect is asking a question. Even a simple question can have a hidden significance. For example: "Do you sell a lot of these?" could get you in trouble if handled the wrong way. If you just say, "yes," you might be surprised to hear, "I'm sorry to hear that. I was looking for something unique."

However, if you say, "Gee, that's an interesting question; why did you ask me that?" the dialogue might continue. The prospect might answer, "Well, because I want to know how many you sell." Then you could say, "That makes sense, but tell me why that is important to you."

When the prospect replies, "Because I'm looking for something unique," you can deal with the issue or suggest an alternative in your answer without getting backed into a corner.

Remember to use softening statements like, "That makes sense," or "That's an interesting question," before your real question so that the prospects don't feel they're being drilled.

7. Turn the tables. In order to maintain control of the sales interview, you have to be the one asking the questions. So remember to turn the tables by ending every answer with another question. Something like, "Does that sound like something you'd be interested in?" or, "Is that a fair statement?" can help you finish qualifying or gather information. Keep the ball rolling at all times, but be natural or you'll sound pushy.

8. Keep in mind that statements aren't questions. If you answer a question that hasn't been asked, you could cause antagonism by sounding like you're defending yourself. This means you have to put your ego aside again, because you won't always agree with your prospect. But it's all part of being a professional.

"It's too expensive!" does not require an answer. It is, however, a sign of resistance. When confronted with resistance, always follow the three *Flowith* steps: (1) Agree. (2) Insert the word *and*. (3) Ask another question (I cover *Flowith* in more detail in Chapter 8).

9. If they ask the same question twice, answer it. You don't want to offend anyone with too many questions. Be sensitive to your prospect's attitudes and facial expressions. A good rule is that if they repeat the same question twice, answer it or it will look like you're ignoring them. But don't be afraid to reject a prospect who refuses to answer any questions or who takes too much of your time to qualify successfully. Part of being a master sales professional lies in knowing that you won't qualify or close every prospect. Rejecting them is sometimes part of maintaining control.

10. Be natural. It's a good idea to hesitate before you answer a question. This shows that you consider the question worthy of thought and helps you avoid sounding like you are working from a script. In all the questioning we suggest in this book, tone and tempo are very important. Practice making them sound natural. Use a mirror or do some role-playing with a colleague.

Your job is to qualify leads as quickly as possible in order either to make an appointment or remove the person or company from your system. An unqualified card or file is an unknown. Develop the attitude that that card needs to prove its value in order to warrant space in your box or computer. Your success will be determined as much by the number of cards you tear up, as by the number of *hot* prospects you have.

Chapter Six Summary

1. Memorize the "Telephone Rules of the Road." They are designed to slide you into a comfortable, productive relationship with your prospects:

   ✗ Have a confident and motivated attitude.

   ✗ Be prepared.

   ✗ Ask for help.

   ✗ Repeat the prospect's first name.

   ✗ Listen actively.

   ✗ Mirror your prospect.

   ✗ Ask qualifying questions.

   ✗ Use the strategic pause.

   ✗ Get specific commitments (up-front contracts).

2. Pay attention to your prospect—and to yourself. Listen to the prospect and monitor your own reactions and behavior.

3. Remember the Ten Rules of Questioning: (1) Most prospects lie. (2) Forget most of the things your mother told you. (3) Put your ego aside. (4) Stop talking your way out of sales—and start questioning your way in. (5) When you're talking, you're not selling. (6) Remember the rule of three. (7) Turn the tables. (8) Keep in mind that statements aren't questions. (9) If they ask the same question twice, answer it. (10) Be natural.

step 2: **establishing rapport**

ESTABLISHING RAPPORT is indisputably one of the most important—and intricate— aspects of the sales interview process. Done correctly and thoroughly, building rapport makes every subsequent step easier and more likely to yield successful results. Conversely, if ignored, the results can be disappointing at best and possibly disas-

trous. It's not a difficult skill to attain, but it does require concentration and timing.

This chapter provides a treasure chest of enlightening information that will give you perspective on the rapport-building process, along with tools, techniques, and some self-administered exercises to help you understand both yourself and the people you are selling to.

Before we begin this chapter on rapport, I invite you, for perspective, to take this two-minute quiz. Take a look at Figure 7-1.

This is *YOU.*

This is YOUR *CUSTOMER.*

FIGURE 7-1

The quiz is a *single* question, and if you answer this question correctly, you will have achieved 90 percent of this chapter's purpose. So again, examine the picture. Look at where you are in the picture.

Note: If you look up into the sky from your side of the world, the selling side, and your customer looks up into the sky from his side of the world, the buying side, *you're looking in opposite directions.*

Now, here's your quiz.

FIGURE 7-2

Quiz Question: From your perspective, how do you go about convincing your customer that your way of looking "UP" is the right way "UP"? *(Please contemplate your response before going on.)*

The traditional sales response is: "Bring the customer 'up' to where you are." This approach is illustrated in Figure 7-2.

The rationale behind this response is: "I need to bring customers to *my side of the world* in order to show them *my way* of looking up."

Is this the *right* response?

The answer is, it's not a question of what's right or wrong. It's a question of what works.

Think about it.

How eager and willing are today's busy consumers to see things from your perspective?

Will your prospects be enthusiastic and excited about trekking all the way to *your side of the world?*

The sad truth is that most consumers don't want to see things from your perspective. They don't care what you have to offer them . . . or what you have to say . . . unless you . . . travel to their side of the world first, as in Figure 7-3.

FIGURE 7-3

Getting Over to Your Customer's Side of the World: An Introduction to Rapport

Most salespeople think that bonding is rapport and that you must bond with the prospect before you can move forward. The difference between bonding and rapport is:

Bonding: Where you, the professional salesperson, do the talking initially to find something in common with the prospects in order to make them feel comfortable about you. You talk and the prospect listens.

Rapport: Where you ask the prospects a question about something positive about them, their company, or their product or service, and they do the talking while you listen, so that you can match, mirror, and pace them. It's getting over to your prospect's side of the world.

The early steps of building rapport with your customers and clients could be the most important and perhaps the most challenging aspects of the sales process.

Your goal at this stage is to create a feeling of similarity between you and your prospect. We are all drawn to those whom we perceive to be like ourselves. To establish rapport, credibility, and trust, you must take the time to set the tone of the call using your matching and mirroring skills.

PRESCRIPTION FOR SUCCESS

Rapport is getting over to your prospect's side of the world.

You might start by asking your prospects to tell you a little bit about themselves and how they got to where they are today. People like to talk about themselves. Your job is to listen. If you are genuine in your interest and enthusiasm, it can be a great rapport builder. If, in the course of listening to the prospect, you find you have something in common, like being from the same town or having gone to the same school, that can also help you.

The following are some ice-breaking suggestions that you may want to use.

SCENARIO ONE

You: I'm glad we were able to talk today. Before we get started, I was wondering if you could share with me some general information about ABC company, such as how long you've been in business, the kind of growth you've been experiencing, and so forth. *Of course, you should know this information already from your pre-call information gathering, as discussed in the previous chapter, but this gives prospects a chance to talk about a subject with which they are familiar.*

Prospect: (Responds)

You: That's very interesting. I wasn't aware that such a large market existed for timesharing. If you don't mind my asking, I'm curious about how you got to your current position as . . .

Or,

You: That's very interesting. I wasn't aware that such a large market existed for timesharing. If you don't mind my asking, I'm always curious about how successful people like yourself got to their current positions. Would you be willing to share that with me?

Prospect: (Responds)

You: Just one last question on that note before we get down to business. If you could pinpoint one quality that you have that has made you unique in how you approach things, what would it be?

SCENARIO TWO

You: Thanks for talking with me today. During the time that we're talking, I'll be asking you some questions. Then there will be a time when you'll ask me some questions, and then we'll decide if we have a basis here for a mutually beneficial relationship. Are you okay with that?

Prospect: Sure.

You: Before we begin the conversation (of course, the conversation has already begun), I wonder if you would share with me a little bit about ABC company, including your role at ABC. How did ABC start? What has been your role in its growth? What is your vision for ABC's future?

Neuro-Linguistic Selling Skills (NLSS)

The use of neuro-linguistics, the study of how people communicate, is a powerful way to subtly create a feeling of similarity between you and your prospect. Different people have different primary communication channels, and if you can identify and tune in to these channels, you can get much better results and shorten the entire sales cycle.

PRESCRIPTION FOR SUCCESS

Neuro-linguistics is the study of how people communicate. Different people have different primary communications channels, and if you can identify and tune in to these channels, you can get much better results and shorten the entire sales cycle.

To understand the study of neuro-linguistics, it is important to first understand the elements of communication. These can be broken down as the following:

55 Percent Physiology
Breathing

Facial expression

Gestures

Matching

Mirroring

Posture

38 Percent Tone
Voice

Tempo

Timbre

Tone

Volume

7 Percent Words
Common experience

Content chunks

Key words and phrases

To give you an illustration of how this breakdown occurs in your own communication, try this exercise: Remember a time when you were a small child and you got in trouble for something you did. The parent or adult who discovered your mischief confronted you. He or she started the reprimand by saying your name. Then, as you looked up at this person and heard the person's voice, you knew instinctively that you were in trouble and why. How come? All the person did was say your name.

Well, as you knew your name, that accounted for 7 percent. But the way your name was said and the posture and expression of the person saying it revealed more to you than the words ever could.

As a matter of fact, I would like to suggest that even as a small child, you unconsciously understood what was going on, maybe not through words, but by using your senses. Children can tell if you are angry, upset, or happy long before they can talk.

The same is true for adults. You don't just hear the words your prospect uses to determine how you are doing on a professional sales interview. How many times have prospects told you that they were really interested but they just had to think it over? You heard what they said, but at the same time, you knew that it was over and they had already decided against it.

When we listen, we are unconsciously picking up information with all of our senses. We express and understand meaning, not only with words but also with mental pictures and tone.

Good communication can be defined by getting the results you want. Neuro-linguistics is a very simple and commonsense sort of science. Its brilliance lies in the way it analyzes and breaks down everyday communication. With an understanding of neuro-linguistics, you can start creating the subtle changes that make a big difference in your ultimate results.

The following are the three main sensory channels that we rely on when communicating and the approximate percentage of the population that relies most on each sense.

Video (seeing): 60 percent

Audio (hearing): 25 percent

Kino (feeling): 15 percent

In addition, there are also the olfactory (smelling) sense, the gustatory (tasting) sense, and intuition. At any given moment, one of these channels is likely to have a greater "signal strength" than the others. We all, however, tend to rely on one sense more than the others.

I believe that intuition is the most powerful sense. Because many people don't understand its importance, it is largely ignored. However, it is becoming much more recognized in some circles, notably in the corporate sector. This will create many changes for big business in the decades to come.

The olfactory sense is extremely powerful in its ability to bring you back to another place or time. No sense can recreate a feeling or memory faster than the sense of smell. For example, have you ever smelled a particular food that your mother used to make? Immediately, your childhood images come to life. You cannot only smell it, but you can see, hear, feel, and taste it. You are literally there! This is a fine example of anchoring in a neuro-linguistic induced state. The increased use of aromatherapy is testimony to how much we've learned about the power of the sense of smell, and about the effectiveness of applying that knowledge.

For the purpose of selling, let's focus on the first three senses: *video, audio,* and *kino.* These are the senses most often used, and most people rely on one more than the others.

The numbers in the list above indicate the approximate percentage of the population that relies more on each sense. As you can see, most people rely most on their video input. They are what we call *primary videos.*

It is important in sales interviews to try to determine which sense your prospects rely on most. In this way you can communicate more effectively by giving them information in the way that they are most responsive to.

For example, primary videos want to *see* your product and *read* your brochures, literature, and testimonials. Primary audios prefer to hear what you have to say about the product and what it can do for them, as well as what other people are saying about it. And primary kinos want to get their hands on your product, try it out, and get the feel of it.

Most people have more than one strategy that they use, but it is important to recognize what their primary one is. For example, if you are a fast-talking visual person and you are trying to communicate with someone who has a primary auditory strategy, you probably won't get through. Remember the teachers you had in school who consistently put you to sleep? They probably were not so much boring as kinesthetic, and their message was falling on your visual or auditory senses.

You can start to type your prospects by listening to the words and phraseology they use. Below are some commonly used words or phrases that people employ to relate their experiences through video, audio, or kino processes.

Video	Audio	Kino
see	hear	sense
look	listen	feel
appear	sounds like	grasp
an eyeful	express yourself	contact
appears to me	idle talk	boils down to
bird's-eye view	loud and clear	cool and calm
clear cut	inquire into	hold it
eye to eye	tuned in	hang in there
in view of	word for word	get the drift
make a scene	unheard of	get in touch

The use of any of these words or phrases does not necessarily indicate a person's sensory channel preference. However, it is important to pay attention to all the words that people use in order to get a general sense of their preference.

Along with what they say (7 percent), you must learn to pay attention to how they say it and to which physiological indicators they are giving you. Here are some guidelines you can follow to identify the three major primary sensory channels as they are used by normally organized, right-handed people.

Primary Video (60 Percent)

Primary video people tend to talk very fast. They use their hands a lot as they speak, and they tend to look up a lot. They think in pictures. They are actually seeing things when they look up.

Remember when you were in school and a teacher exclaimed, "The answer is not on the ceiling!" Well, for primary video students, the answer was on the ceiling. In general, videos look up and to their right when they create and up and to their left when they remember.

Their breathing is shallow or very high up in their chest, and when they get excited, they may almost hyperventilate. They say things like, "I see," "I get the picture," "It looks good," and "That's not what I envision."

They usually make quick decisions. They tend to be very neat dressers and are concerned about the appearance of everything. Their desks and living areas tend to be neat and orderly. They also have a tendency to believe what they read, or what they see you do.

Primary Audio (24 Percent)

Primary audio people tend to talk at a moderate rate. Strangely, their voices are usually more monotonous than primary video people. In general, they are very even tempered. They don't get too excited, and their manner and breathing are more even and relaxed.

Primary audios would probably read things out loud or repeat them over and over again when studying for an exam. They talk to themselves and hear things in their mind.

They tend to look from side to side a lot as they think and speak. In general, they look to their right when they are creating and to their left when they are remembering. They think across as if they are reading the words.

They say things like, "I like the sound of that," "That rings a bell," "Tell me more," and "I don't think I'm hearing you correctly." They have a tendency to believe what you say and what they hear.

Primary Kino (15 Percent)

Primary kinos are probably the most misunderstood of the three types of people. They tend to talk very slowly. Their tone and timbre are very soft. They are used to getting cut off when they speak because people don't want to wait for them to finish.

They are very mellow. They have to get a feel for things before they act, so they may take a long time to make decisions. Some people might mistakenly think that they're less intelligent. They are no less intelligent; they just communicate differently.

Kinos are more in touch with their intuition than any other group. They therefore tend to take things personally, and their feelings are hurt more easily than others. They feel the weight of the world on their shoulders. They have to deal with life's pressures.

A kino person's first reaction in a crisis is to feel terrible. They say things like, "I have to get a handle on the situation," "My feeling is this," and "I'm beginning to grasp the idea."

They look down and to the right a lot. They breathe from deep down in their diaphragm. They tend to wear comfortable clothing and surround themselves with comfortable furniture and belongings. They like to touch and be touched, and, in general, they are very warm, gentle, caring people.

Now that you have a basic understanding of the range of behavior that you can encounter, think about how your communication with different types of people can be affected.

A video or audio person who is not responsive to the methods of a kino undoubtedly finds it difficult and perhaps even unpleasant to communicate with one. And the reverse is true as well.

In sales, our job is to communicate freely and effectively with all types of people. We can do this by mirroring and matching.

Eye Watching

Eye movements are linked to the kind of sensory processing that is going on in a person at any given moment. Presently, the neuro-linguistic "model" is based only on observations, and no experimental proof yet exists for the suggested link between the eyes and the brain's sensory-processing mechanisms.

Figure 7-4 reveals eye patterns and readings for a right-handed person in the neuro-linguistic view. The eye movement may be only a bare flicker, or it may be held for several seconds. The individual may be organizing incoming current sensations, recalling others from the past, or imagining still others never previously experienced. In all cases, one gets clues about whether the mode of processing is video, audio, or kino (involving stimuli generated within the body itself) by watching the eyes.

Eyes up and to the left. Recalling something seen before: A Video memory.

Eyes up and to the right: Visualizing something that has *not been seen before.*

Eyes staring into space and not focused, with some pupil dilation: Either Video recall or visualizing something that has never been seen before.

Eyes horizontal, looking right or left: Making sense of sounds one is hearing at the moment, recalling sounds from memory, or imagining sounds; Audio processing.

Eyes down and to the right: Sensing how the body feels; processing Kino input.

Eyes down and to the left: Talking to oneself; an internal dialogue in the Audio mode.

FIGURE 7-4

When you are able to determine your prospects' primary sensory channel, you will be able to adapt your communication to *their* personal style. Give them what they respond to best. Show them, tell them, or help them get a feeling for your subject. Ask them questions that show you understand how they think and the processes they have to go through. "What would you have to see in order to make your decision today?" Talk to them on *their* level and they'll want to work with you and refer you to others.

Now that you have a basic understanding of the range of behavior you can run across, think about how communication with different types of people can be affected. You can do this by *mirroring* and *matching*.

Mirroring and Matching

If we try to create rapport with only the content of our conversation, we are missing out on one of the biggest ways we can communicate similarity to another person. That is mirroring, which is the act of adopting another person's behavior as if you were that person's mirror image.

Mirroring requires two things from you: keen attention and personal flexibility. On the telephone, it means that you must be able to identify and match peoples' verbal attitudes, their expressions, tone of voice, and forms of speech. If done subtly, you will be able to create a strong sense of rapport between yourself and the other people.

This has two payoffs. As you mirror both speech and physiology, the person being mirrored is thinking, "Hey, this guy is like me! He must be okay!"

Second, mirroring literally gives you the opportunity to put yourself briefly into their shoes and allows you to communicate with them from *their side of the world*.

When you first talk to people, ask them a question and pay attention to how they respond. You will eventually use your neuro-linguistic information to try and classify them, but start by just mirroring them without understanding their entire process. If they talk slowly, do the same. If they speak softly, so will you. Get their attention, make a connection, and then slowly resume your normal pattern. If you find you are losing their attention, go back and mirror them again. In this way, you will form a solid bond with your prospect. Once that bond is formed, it's okay to be yourself.

PRESCRIPTION FOR SUCCESS

When you first talk to people, ask them a question and pay attention to how they respond. You will eventually use your neuro-linguistic information to try and classify them, but start by just mirroring them without understanding their entire process.

Mirror your prospect's vocabulary, rate of speech, phrase construction, volume, and mood to help develop stronger bonds. We all prefer to do business with people we feel are more like us. We communicate best with friends, significant others, and business associates who see the world the way we do.

By paying closer attention to the way your prospects and customers communicate, you are able to show that you understand their situation and unique business needs. You can demonstrate that awareness by mirroring and selectively matching their phrase construction, volume, vocabulary, rhythm, and mood.

PHRASE CONSTRUCTION

Listen carefully to the pattern of the prospects' speech and respond in kind. Some people speak in short, choppy sentences, while others talk in long, drawn-out phrases. If prospects interrupt you frequently, one reason may be that they think in short phrases and are impatient with the length of your sentences. Try shortening your sentences. If prospects repeatedly ask you for more explanations, they are probably more comfortable with longer, more detailed thoughts, and you should communicate in kind.

VOLUME

Keep your volume level close to that of the person on the other end of the line. Many professional sales reps make a common mistake by shouting at customers when trying to get them to talk louder. What usually happens is that prospects respond by lowering their voices to get the salesperson to hear them and listen!

The result is frustration on both ends of the line.

If you lower your volume to match that of someone who is soft spoken, that person will feel more comfortable conversing with you!

Never automatically assume that older prospects have hearing problems. Raising your voice may only offend them.

VOCABULARY

Listen to and repeat the words your prospect uses, whether or not they are appropriate. Be willing to speak their language. In selling a service or product to a computer enthusiast, for example, you will use an entirely different vocabulary from what you would use when you sell the same thing to an avid sports fan.

The best way to find your way around your prospects' working vocabulary is through the creative use of open-ended questions and active listening skills. Write down key words and phrases as they speak and use them appropriately throughout the conversation. Keep notes about the customers' word choices and conversation styles on your information cards for callbacks.

That way, you can begin the next conversation on the same positive note as the last one.

RHYTHM AND RATE OF SPEECH

To be in better sync with your prospects, adjust your rhythm and rate of speech to theirs. We all believe that we speak at a "normal" rate of speech, not always understanding how prospects make many subconscious value judgments about salespeople they can't see based on how quickly or slowly they speak. By mirroring your prospects' speech rate, you avoid any such preconceived judgments that can interfere with building rapport.

MOODS

Without adopting the mood of your prospects, match the pace of your energy to theirs. If you are bubbly and bouncy when you place a call to those who are downcast and depressed, you won't establish rapport. In fact, they might even hang up. By briefly pacing and matching their low energy level, however, you will be more flexible in giving support until you can subtly shift energy to alter their mood.

When you are able to determine your prospects' primary sensory channel, you will be able to adapt your communication strategy to their personal style. Give them what they will respond to best. Create pictures for them, explain and define things for them, or help them get a feeling for your subject.

PRESCRIPTION FOR SUCCESS

When you are able to determine your prospect's primary sensory channel, you will be able to adapt your communication strategy to their personal style... and get over to their side of the world!

Ask them questions that show you understand how they think and the processes they have to go through: "What would you have to see in order to make your decision today?"

Talk to them on *their* level—from *their* side of the world—and they'll want to work with you and refer you to others.

Although this section provides a good overview of neuro-linguistics, I highly recommend that you study this science further in order to make the best use of it. Neuro-linguistics can be both fascinating and useful for your personal and professional life.

Have fun using this valuable new tool!

■ ■

The Five-Minute Sales Boost Exercise

While understanding the primary communication mode of your prospects and clients is important in relating to them effectively, understanding your own preferences is crucial to being able to maximize your potential in dealing with others.

The following exercise is designed to help you uncover your primary mode of communicating. This is not a test in the sense that there are any right or wrong answers. That is, don't spend any time wondering which choice you *should* be making.

When you have finished, you may have gained some insight into what makes you tick and have taken a step toward becoming a powerful salesperson.

The exercise contains three parts.

PART 1

Instructions: Part 1 consists of five sets of three paragraphs each. For each set, select the one paragraph that is easiest for you to read. Do not be concerned with the actual content of the paragraph, merely with how you *respond* to it compared to the other paragraphs in the set.

Read all three paragraphs and then make your selection, but do not deliberate too long. Your first response generally is best. Indicate the letter of the paragraph that you have selected on your answer sheet by circling the appropriate letter (A, B, or C) for each set.

Take no more than five minutes to complete each exercise.

1. A. The tinkle of the wind chimes tells me that the breeze is still rustling outside. In the distance, I can hear the whistle of the train.

   B. I can see the rows of flowers in the yard, their colors shining and fading in the sunlight and shadows, their petals woven in the breeze.

   C. As I ran, I could feel the breeze on my back. My feet pounded along the path. The blood raced through my veins, and I felt very alert.

2. A. I like to be warm. On a cold night, I like to relax by a warm fire in a comfortable room with a cup of smooth, warm cocoa and a fuzzy blanket.

   B. The child talked into the toy telephone as though he were calling a friend. Listening to the quiet conversation, I could almost hear the ethos of another child, long ago.

   C. The view was magnificent. It was one of the most beautiful things I have ever seen. The panorama of the green countryside stretched out clearly below us in the bright, sparkling sun.

3. A. They appeared to be surprised when they noticed that there were other people on the beach. The amazement on their faces turned to eagerness as they looked to see if they knew any of the people on the sand.

B. I was helped up and supported until I felt my strength coming back. The tingling sensation that ran up and down my legs—especially in my body—was extremely warm.

C. People will express themselves more verbally if they can talk about their interests or assets. You can hear the increased enthusiasm in their conversations, and they usually become more silent.

4. A. The feedback that the speaker received was an indication that she was communicating more effectively. The people in the audience seemed to be tuned into what she was talking about.

B. I want to understand how people feel in their inner worlds, to accept them, as they feel free to think, feel, and be anything they desire.

C. Children watch adults. They notice more than we realize. You can see this if you observe them at play. They mimic the behavior of the grown-ups they see.

5. A. Creative, artistic people have an eye for beauty. They see patterns and forms that other people do not notice. They respond to the colors around them, and their visual surroundings can affect their moods.

B. They heard the music as if for the first time. Each change of tone and tempo caught their ears. The sounds soared throughout the room, while the rhythms echoed in their heads.

C. Everybody was stirred by the deep emotions generated by the interaction. Some felt subdued and experienced it quietly. Others were stimulated and excited. They all felt alert to each new sensation.

PART 2

Instructions: This part consists of ten sets of items. Each item includes three lists (sets) of words. For each item, circle the letter (A, B, or C) of the set of words that is easiest for you to read. Do not focus on the meanings of the words. Try to work quickly.

6. A. Witness   B. Interview   C. Sensation
      Look   Listen   Touch
      See   Hear   Feel

7. A. Stir   B. Watch   C. Squeal
      Sensitive   Scope   Remark
      Hustle   Pinpoint   Discuss

8. A. Proclaim   B. Texture   C. Exhibit
      Mention   Handle   Inspect
      Acoustic   Tactile   Vista

9. A. Scrutinize   B. Articulate   C. Exhilarate
      Focused   Hearken   Support
      Scene   Tone   Grip

10. A. Ringing   B. Movement   C. Glitter
      Hearsay   Heat   Mirror
      Drumbeat   Rushing   Outlook

11. A. Dream   B. Listen   C. Motion
      Glow   Quiet   Soft
      Illusion   Silence   Tender

12. A. Upbeat   B. Firm   C. Bright
      Listen   Hold   Appear
      Record   Concrete   Picture

13. A. Feeling   B. Hindsight   C. Hearsay
      Lukewarm   Purple   Audible
      Muscle   Book   Horn

14. A. Show   B. Tempo   C. Move
     Observant   Articulate   Powerful
     Glimpse   Sonar   Reflex

15. A. Purring   B. Smooth   C. Glowing
     Overhear   Grasp   Lookout
     Melody   Relaxed   Vision

PART 3

Instructions: This part consists of ten sets of three short phrases each. In each set, circle the letter (A, B, or C) of the phrase that you find easiest to read. Try to complete this task in the time remaining.

16. A. An eyeful   B. An earful   C. A handful

17. A. Lend me an ear   B. Give him a hand   C. Keep an eye out

18. A. Hand in hand   B. Eye to eye   C. Word for word

19. A. Get the picture   B. Hear the word   C. Come to grips with

20. A. The thrill of the chase   B. A flash of lightning   C. The roll of thunder

21. A. Outspoken   B. Underhanded   C. Shortsighted

22. A. I see   B. I hear you   C. I get it

23. A. Hang in there   B. Bird's-eye view   C. Rings true

24. A. Clear as a bell   B. Smooth as silk   C. Bright as day

25. A. Look here   B. Listen up   C. Catch this

SCORING INSTRUCTIONS

Now, transfer the letters you have circled for each question to the sheet below, entering the letter chosen opposite the appropriate question number.

	Kino	Visual	Audio		Kino	Visual	Audio
1.	C	B	A	14.	C	A	B
2.	A	C	B	15.	B	C	A
3.	B	A	C	16.	C	A	B
4.	B	C	A	17.	B	C	A
5.	C	A	B	18.	A	B	C
6.	C	A	B	19.	C	A	B
7.	A	B	C	20.	A	B	C
8.	B	C	A	21.	B	C	A
9.	C	A	B	22.	C	A	B
10.	B	C	A	23.	A	B	C
11.	C	A	B	24.	B	C	A
12.	B	C	A	25.	C	A	B
13.	A	B	C				

Next, total the letters circled in each vertical column. Place the three totals in the space below. Then multiply each total by four to obtain your actual score.

Kino Column _____ × by 4 = _____ (Actual Score)

Visual Column _____ × by 4 = _____ (Actual Score)

Audio Column _____ × by 4 = _____ (Actual Score)

Chart your scores on the graph below by coloring in the space that represents your actual score in each of the three columns.

	10	20	30	40	50	60	70	80	90	100
Auditory Column 3										
Visual Column 2										
Kinesthetic Column 1										

EXERCISE SUMMARY

Your highest score indicates the primary mode that you use to interpret and communicate with the world around you. You probably use this mode the most (auditory, visual, or kinesthetic) when you are problem solving or in stressful situations.

Your second highest (middle) score indicates your secondary mode, which you likely use in everyday conversation in combination with your primary mode.

Your lowest score indicates your tertiary mode, which you likely do not use as much as the other two, or at all, in your normal conversation. In fact, it often remains at the unconscious level.

These three modes of perceiving and talking about one's experience are called a language representation system. An audio person is likely to say, "I hear you," or "That sounds right." A kinesthetic person is more likely to say, "I've got it," or "That feels right." The items that you selected during this exercise reflect these three systems or ways of describing experiences.

Each individual seems to be most comfortable in using one or two of these systems. Some people believe, however, that if an individual could learn to communicate in all three modes, or systems, that person could establish more rapport and trust with people whose primary systems differ from his or her own. Increased ability to communicate in all three systems might therefore lead to increased *effectiveness* in communication.

Five-Minute Sales Boost Exercise #2

The following exercise is another simple way for you to identify your primary representational system. The exercise has four parts. Give yourself a few minutes to get comfortable, and then begin.

PART 1

1. Get a piece of paper and a pen.
2. Imagine a man sitting by a fire with a book on his lap. His hand, draped over the chair arm, rests on the head of a large

dog. There is a stereo/rack system clearly visible in the background, with CDs stacked all around it. When you look outside the window, snow is falling.

3. Describe what the man is doing in five words or less. Yes, that's right. No more than five words. You have two minutes.

PART 2

On the back of your paper, write down the words in the following list to which you react the strongest:

Rush	Risk	Rasp	Colorful	Ache
Emerald	Rainbow	Warm	Glorious	Strident
Rustling	Whispering	Blinding	Trembling	Sunset
Thunderous	Powerful	Silent	Gentle	Mirage
Hearken	Grasping	Huge	Lightening	Laughing

PART 3

Take a moment and imagine yourself taking a walk in your town. Perhaps you live in the city or the suburbs. Wherever you live, imagine what talking a walk for several minutes might be like. On a clean piece of paper, describe what you see, what you experience, and what you hear.

PART 4

Below are excerpts from three well-known poems. Pick which set of words (A, B, or C) you can identify with the most and which moves you, stirs you, and connects with you emotionally.

Set A

Within the shadow of the ship
I watched their rich attire:
Blue, glossy green, and velvet black
They coiled and swam and every track
Was a flash of golden fire.

Set B

Keeping time, time, time,

In a sort of Runic rhyme,

To the tintinnabulation that so musically wells

From the bells, bells, bells, bells, bells, bells, bells"

Set C

Oh Western wind, when wilt thou blow,

That the small rain down can rain?

Christ, that my love were in my arms,

And I in my bed again.

THE RESULTS

Again, we have three ways of sensing, interpreting, and acting on what surrounds us: auditory (what we hear), visual (what we see), and kinesthetic (what we sense, or feel). One of these traits is dominant in your personality. Turn over the sheet with your responses to the preceding exercise and put the headings "Auditory," "Visual," and "Kinesthetic" across the top. Since you were allowed only five words or less to describe what the man was doing, you would have written something that would fall into one of the three categories.

Review your response. Did you write something like "listening to CDs"? If so, then put a check mark under *Auditory*. If you wrote something like, "reading a book" or "watching the fire," put a check under *Visual*. But if you wrote, "petting the dog" or "warming himself by the fire," then put a check mark under *Kinesthetic*.

In Part 1, you circled words that caused you some reaction. Look at all of the circled words. Are most of them "rustling, rasp, silent, laughing"? If so, then they go under your *Auditory* heading. If you chose words like "emerald, lightning, mirage, and rainbow," then put these words under your *Visual* heading. If most of your words were more like "powerful, grasping, warm, and ache," you need to put them under the *Kinesthetic* heading.

For Part 3, you chose a 100-word description of your walk. Review the types of words you used most often. For example, if you referenced sights often, then put those words under *Visual*. If you referenced sounds, put those words under *Auditory*, and likewise for sensations, under *Kinesthetic*.

In Part 4, the excerpts from poems, here's what your choice looks like: If you chose Set A, then you are visual. If you chose Set B, you are auditory, and if you chose Set C, you are kinesthetic.

The important thing to remember is that it takes all kinds of people to make the world go around. There is no right or wrong style. Once you are able to identify your personality style, it will help you to better understand how you process information.

PRESCRIPTION FOR SUCCESS

Once you are able to identify your personality style, it will help you to better understand how you process information.

When you begin to identify these traits in other people, like your prospects, for instance, you will be able to better communicate with them, which will make the process of building a relationship with them less overwhelming and a lot less confusing.

By discovering all of the things that make you the way you are, you are more apt to notice the "telltale signs" about your prospective clients that let you know exactly what they are experiencing.

For example, the next time you have a meeting, take an "inventory" of what people around the room are doing.

✗ Do you see people wandering around the room with their eyes?

✗ Are people expressionless and listless?

✗ Perhaps the guy in the corner has been doodling on his napkin for fifteen minutes while you were giving your presentation.

When people are not stimulated by the primary style, they become antsy and uninterested.

If you are speaking with visual people, don't bore them with stacks of statistical data. Give them a chart with multiple colors. They need to connect with the pictures because that's their style. They need to be stimulated with objects, not numbers.

Likewise, if you are meeting with "warm and fuzzy" types, they need to feel like you are all connecting before they can even start talking about business. Rushing into your presentation will turn them off quickly. Ask them a lot of questions. Find out what they are thinking about, and gradually show them your information to help them "connect" with you during the presentation. Their eye contact, nodding of the head, and facial expressions will let you know what's going on inside their heads.

Just because you have a primary personality trait doesn't mean that, depending on the circumstances, you won't slip back and forth between other traits. Every one of us has a primary, secondary, and tertiary personality style. Sometimes it depends on what's happening to us at a given moment.

And if that were true for us as salespeople, wouldn't it be true for prospective clients as well?

PRESCRIPTION FOR SUCCESS

The best way to understand others is to first understand yourself.

Neuro-Linguistic Review
SELLING TO AN AUDITORY PROSPECT

Use testimonials and endorsements. Since they think with words rather than pictures and feelings, they are strongly interested in, and likely to be impressed by, word-for-word quotations and citations.

Mirror their way of speaking. Copy their pacing, tone, vocabulary, and volume, but not so obviously that they know they're being imitated.

Vary tone, pitch, volume, and speech rate to emphasize and verbally punctuate your most important points. Auditory people pay as much attention to how you speak as to what you say.

Sprinkle in audio-oriented words: "Does that *sound good* to you?" "Are we in *harmony* on that point?" "Do I need to *amplify* anything we've covered?"

In addition to visual or print brochures, which often end up lying around unread or being thrown away, send audio customers and prospects informational and descriptive cassette tapes or CDs. They'll play them out of curiosity alone.

Call them on the phone frequently. Even a brief conversation can revive interest or serve as a clincher.

SELLING TO A VISUAL PROSPECT

With these people, even mental pictures really are worth a thousand words! In addition, visual materials can be sent from afar, such as physical objects and samples, or charts, graphs, photos, slides, and videotapes.

Rely on visual expressions: "Does this *look good* to you?" "Have I made that *clear?*" "*Imagine* what that could mean to your company."

In your close, lead your prospect through a review of benefits as though broadcasting a television drama. Use their imagination to picture the agreement you've reached. As you verbalize these benefits, make sure the prospects "see" the contract in their mind's eye.

Speaking artfully, carefully, and creating mental images is crucial to impress highly visual people with your professionalism and to succeed with them.

SELLING TO A KINESTHETIC PROSPECT

Use words that suggest physical action and emotional words: "How do you *feel* about the proposal?" "Are you *comfortable* with these options?" "I want to get a *handle* on your exact requirements."

Since you can't establish physical contact, use words that bring you emotionally closer to the prospects and that create positive feelings about your product, so that they will perceive you as genuine, caring, and sincere. As the commercial says, "Reach out and touch someone." If you choose your words carefully, the kinesthetic prospects will intuitively know that you care very much about what you say.

PRESCRIPTION FOR SUCCESS

1. Notice those people, in both personal and professional relationships, with whom you are in rapport and those with whom you are out of rapport. What is the difference between the two sets of people?

2. What do you need to know about an individual in order to want to be in rapport with him? Are there people you work with daily with whom you are continually out of rapport? What specifically makes it difficult for you to be with these people? What would they have to do or think differently for you to accept them? Consider behaviors you would have to adopt in order to accept them.

3. Examine your client base. Are these people you have a difficult time with? Consider any nonverbal similarities you could gravitate toward (volume, tone, tempo, pitch, and cadence) to help you create rapport with them.

4. During your calls, get into a voice match immediately through your volume, tone, tempo, pitch, and cadence. Although this is a conscious process for you, the person on the other end won't notice anything other than a feeling of sameness. (It is not necessary to continue with the match throughout the call, just until criterial rapport is reached.)

5. You will recognize rapport when the conversation takes on an easy flow and you are aware, or unconscious, of trying to do anything different than be who you are. Note in several conversations how long it takes you to get into rapport. Are there time differences between conversations with people you know and cold calls?

6. Maintain a "we space" by working from agreement and continually summing up the information you've gathered.

7. Internally, continually monitor your client's comfort level. Has his tempo changed? The volume? Are the two of you regularly taking turns speaking? Is he getting interested enough in you to ask you questions?

Chapter 7 Summary

Create rapport at the earliest moment during a call; in other words, get over to your prospect's side of the world. Ask open-ended questions and listen.

Remember—words make up only 7 percent of communications.

And 38 percent of communication is the *tone* conferred by the prospect's voice.

PAY ATTENTION TO TEMPO, TIMBRE, TONE, AND VOLUME

Physiology matters, even though you and the prospect are not face-to-face.

1. Pay attention to your own physiology: your posture and facial expressions. These will come across in your voice, and . . .

2. You will be able to sense the physiology of the person you are talking to through the clues in their voice.

Through *mirroring* and using audio language clues, determine whether your prospect is a *primary video*, a *primary audio*, or a *primary kino* and adapt your language accordingly.

Use mirroring and matching both to create rapport and to reinforce it, once you've established it.

Key Functions

Phrase construction

Volume

Vocabulary

Rhythm/rate of speech

Mood

The *old* game of sales—persuasion, manipulation, frustration, and control (it takes a lot of work to get your customers over to your side of the world)—works for both you *and* your customers.

The new game of pressure-free selling—connection, inquiry, communication, and commitment—also takes a lot of work to get to your customer's side of the world, but at least you're not burdening someone you hardly know.

step 3: finding the pain

LET'S PRETEND that you go to see a doctor for a checkup one day, and when you get there, the doctor says, "Boy am I glad you're here today—we've got a special on kidney stone removal—whaddaya say?" You answer, "But Doc, my kidneys are fine."

And the doctor says, "Oh, really? Well how about a tonsillectomy—we're running

a special on that, too, and boy do we do good work. I mean ask anyone! How about it?" By now, you'd probably be looking for the door.

Obviously, the doctor didn't bother to ask what you needed before trying to sell you things you didn't need. Sound crazy? But what do we do as sales professionals all the time?

Forget what other people have told you. Don't begin a sales interview with your presentation. Why?

Because it's the same as a doctor recommending a cure before diagnosing the ailment.

When calling a prospect, think of yourself as a *sales doctor.*

Remember that people don't buy to get features or benefits. The real reason they buy is to alleviate or avoid pain. As soon as prospects realize that you have the cure for the pain, they'll close the sale themselves.

Instead of making a presentation, ask questions, following a very specific sequence.

1. First, you want to find the pain—the prospect's problem.

2. Then you want to qualify the patient or prospect.

3. Finally, you want to propose the cure (make the presentation).

Never make the presentation until you've gone through the first two steps. Do it too soon, and the patient may not die, but the sale will!

The Sales Doctor® approach is the most powerful and effective method of selling today. All it requires is good questioning skills and an understanding of a very basic concept.

Highly effective sales professionals know how to examine their prospects the way a doctor would. They find the pain, make a diagnosis, write a prescription, and start a treatment plan. You'd be amazed how little time most sales professionals and entrepreneurs really spend on asking prospects about their needs, their problems, and their concerns. Play doctor with your prospects and see how they respond. You'll soon see how this simple technique can make all the difference in your results.

Finding the Pain

Think of yourself as the sales doctor from the very beginning of the call. Start with the kind of conversation that puts the prospect at ease and establishes rapport. Then question the prospect just as a doctor would question a patient to uncover and diagnose the symptoms.

Ask open-ended questions, such as, "How is your present system (or service)?" Depending on the answers you get, move from there to specifics—perhaps: "What don't you like about it?" or "What problems have you had?" or "If you could change one thing, what would it be?"

As the prospect answers these questions, listen to the answers. One of the biggest mistakes most sales professionals make is talking too much. If you're talking, you're out of control. Worse than that, you're not selling.

As the prospects answer your questions, they begin to reveal their pain. But don't be too quick to propose a treatment or cure. You still don't have enough information to work with; you need to dig and probe with even more questions. The surgeon's tool is the scalpel, and the sales professional's tools are types of questions that are designed to get the prospect to open up. Just as a doctor would ask you questions about your condition, you need to question your prospects about their situations.

Ask, "Is there anything else you need to tell me?" or "You mentioned your concern about (whatever). Can you tell me a little more about that?"

Keep digging. Keep probing.

Here are some other questions that may be useful:

✗ "How long have you been looking for . . .?"

✗ "Is size important?"

✗ "Do you have any particular concerns relating to . . .?"

✗ "Is there anything about your present system that you particularly like?"

✗ "Is there anything you particularly dislike?"

Sometimes your prospects (patients) may not realize that they have a problem or pain. In these cases, it is necessary to probe for the pain. If you were selling testing kits, for example, it might sound something like this:

SCENARIO ONE

You: How is your present testing system working for you?

Prospect: Fine.

You: When you say "fine," what, specifically, do you mean?

Prospect: Well, the tests are inaccurate sometimes, but overall, they're okay.

You: So, if they were more precise, you'd be completely happy with it? Is that a fair statement?

Prospect: Well, no.

You: Why not?

Prospect: Well, after we catch an error, the next twenty or so tests require extra checking, which means doing them over.

You: Oh, I see. What happens when you do the tests over?

Prospect: Well, it takes time. Sometimes it's messy, and it takes longer to get the job done.

You: Gee, how do you feel when that happens?

Prospect: Terrible! The real work isn't getting done because they're playing with the equipment! And the boss thinks they're poorly managed and goofing off.

Now that you finally know the real pain, prepare yourself and the prospect for the presentation (operation) by asking:

You: If you could wave a magic wand and create the perfect test, what would you like? What would it do for you personally to help you do your job?

SCENARIO TWO

You: How is your present testing system working for you?

Prospect: Fine.

You: When you say "fine," what specifically, do you mean?

Prospect: It works fine. I'm happy with it.

You: Let me ask you this. On a scale from 0 to 10, 10 being highest, how productive would you say your testing system is?

Prospect: I'd give it an 8.

You: What would it take for the system to be a 10?"

Prospect: Well, it would have to be a system that didn't fail so often and wouldn't require much checking and calibration.

You: Oh, I see. It sounds like you don't have that kind of system now. Is that a fair statement?

Prospect: Yes, that's fair to say.

You: How do you feel about losing 20 percent in productivity?

Prospect: Not too good. It's probably costing me money in the long run.

You: If there were a cost-effective way to bring your testing and productivity up to 10, would that interest you?

Prospect: Why, sure. Anybody would be interested in that.

After uncovering three or more areas of pain that your prospect may have, it is important to determine the intensity of each pain. In other words, what hurts most, least, and in between. It might sound something like this:

You: In order for me to be sure that I have all of this straight, let me go over this list of concerns with you again. You are upset about the frequent failure rate. The service tech usually doesn't get there until the next day to check the equipment. The system isn't designed to handle emergency requirements, so you end up sending material out for testing. And, except for one person, no one can really figure out how to operate the calibrator. Do I have it straight?

Prospect: Yes.

You: Okay. And which of those issues is the greatest concern to you?

Continue in this manner until you have the prospect's concerns in order of his or her priorities.

A QUICK EXAMPLE

Steve Henderson landed a great sales job working for a leader in the packaged goods food industry. One of his first sales calls was with a buyer from a major supermarket chain. Steve wanted to convince the buyer to take on a line extension that the food company was introducing. Steve had enjoyed many years as a successful salesperson and used a "tried and true" presentation with lots of bells and whistles, plenty of audiovisual props, and a stack of statistics.

This sales strategy had helped Steve rack in tons of new clients for previous employers. He even got salesman of the year for three years in a row.

When Steve gave his presentation to the buyer, the buyer appeared to be a little uncomfortable during Steve's pitch. Steve assumed his uncomfortable attitude was attributable to the fact that Steve was new and that the buyer was used to a different sales rep.

At the end of his presentation, the buyer asked Steve a few questions, and when Steve asked for the sale, the buyer said he'd get back to him. The buyer never did. Steve's attempts to "touch base" with the buyer were intercepted by voicemail or an administrative assistant. Steve tried reaching the buyer at an off time to see if he could catch him before the start of the workday, and he did. The buyer politely said he really didn't have the shelf space for the new line, so the decision would be on the back burner for a while.

After some reflection, Steve discovered his mistake. It occurred to Steve that he might have overwhelmed the buyer or come off too strongly during the presentation, and perhaps the buyer really needed a different type of approach.

Steve knew he had let his anxiety prevent him from paying attention to the buyer's nonverbal messages and listening attentively to the buyer's needs.

Steve remembered that the sales manager had mentioned prior to this presentation that shelf space was tight, but Steve neglected to focus on this critical pain point for the buyer and instead went in for the kill, so to speak. He was more concerned with closing the deal than he was with understanding the buyer's needs and providing a solution for the buyer's pain point.

Steve realized he should have prepared a presentation around the *pain point* and negotiated for the space. Once he got his thoughts together, he sat down and wrote the buyer a letter. The letter was centered on solving the major pain point the buyer had—the shelf space. In the letter, Steve referenced several trade deals that his company had previously used for line extensions that proved to be real benefits for retailers. When the buyer called a few days later and asked Steve for a follow-up meeting, Steve was able to seal the deal successfully.

PRESCRIPTION FOR SUCCESS

There are no cookie cutter sales techniques that are guaranteed to work every time. If you thoughtfully and genuinely take your clients' or prospects' pain points into consideration and you are prepared to answer their questions about the challenges they face, you will be positioned for sales success.

If Steve had done his homework the first time around, he would have put together a simple presentation that demonstrated the benefits of the line expansion and would have immediately provided examples to the buyer to accommodate the change. When Steve let his anxiety drive his thought process, his "pump and circumstance" sales strategy kicked in, and it was obviously not the way to approach this buyer.

Because Steve's strategy had worked before, he used it as a fall-back for an uncomfortable presentation.

Often when anxiety kicks in, we cling to behavior that is familiar, but in the case of sales, this familiarity can be a gateway to disaster. All potential or existing customers need to have their needs addressed in a way that is unique to their circumstances.

Turning the Tables

When you go to a doctor, your first question is usually, "What's wrong with me, Doc?" More often than not, doctors won't answer you right away. Instead, they ask you a question in return: "Good question. Where does it hurt?" By doing this, they get more information from you. You talk more specifically about your pain. The technique of answering a question with a question is called *turning the tables.*

When working with your prospects, you have to be more of a specialist than a general practitioner. The question that the prospect asks is never the real question. (Remember the rule of three.) In order to uncover the real problem, the specialist (sales professional) has to move the patient (prospect) through at least two levels of questioning, or turning the tables.

The first question that the prospect asks is usually intellectual in nature. As you turn the tables and ask a question about the question, prospects will think you don't understand, and they will rephrase the question. As they rephrase the question, it becomes more specific, but they are still functioning on the intellectual level, so you turn the tables again. The next rephrasing will usually be the real question. It might sound something like this:

> **Prospect:** How is your company different from your competition? (intellectual question)
>
> **You:** Good question. What, specifically, do you mean by different? (first turn)

Prospect: Well, how fast does your service department respond? (intellectual question)

You: It sounds like fast response is important to you. Is that a fair statement? (second turn)

Prospect: It sure is. I don't want to get stuck with poor service again. (Aha!)

So why should you turn the tables on a question? Here are four very good reasons:

1. To discover the real question behind a particular problem

2. To stay in control of the interview

3. To avoid giving the wrong information

4. To avoid falling into a black hole

The following is an example of the kind of black hole that sales professionals allow themselves to fall into:

Prospect: Does this unit print out multiple result sheets?

You: It sure does. You have a choice of five, ten, fifteen, or twenty copies at a clip. Which operation would you like to see first?

Prospect: None. I don't want multiple copies.

However, if you use turning-the-table skills, it might sound like this:

Prospect: Does this unit print out multiple results? (intellectual question)

You: Good question. Is that important to you? (first turn)

Prospect: I was just wondering if multiple printouts were an option, or if it's built into the unit? (intellectual question)

You: That's a good point. Can I ask you why it matters? (second turn)

Prospect: Yes. It's a waste of money. I don't want every clerk in my lab making extra copies just in case one happens to be a little off-center. (Aha!)

You: That's a very good point. Do you think you would be okay with a copier that had a multiple printout capability that could only be used with discretion?

Prospect: Well, yes. That would make a lot of sense.

Be Gentle, Doctor

No one likes to go to a doctor who treats people roughly. Even if the doctor is a technical genius, patients won't go if they feel they're not being listened to or are being manhandled.

Sales doctors need to be gentle, too. There are two ways to ask questions: abrasively and gently. Your job is to ask a question in response to their question—gently and in a nurturing fashion. Each question responded to needs to be prefaced by a nurturing statement that first acknowledges the prospect's question. Start your questions with phrases such as:

"That's a good point."

"Good question."

"I'm glad you asked that."

"That makes sense."

"I appreciate you asking me that."

Be Precise

Many of the objections that prospects raise are vague. Try to get the prospect to be specific by memorizing and using the following reverses:

Prospect: All of these products are alike.

You: All of them?

Prospect: This product is too expensive.

You: Compared to what?

Prospect: I don't need a lot of bells and whistles.

You: When you say bells and whistles, what specifically do you mean?

Prospect: Your presentation doesn't make sense.

You: How, specifically, doesn't it make sense?

Prospect: I can't make a decision about that today.

You: Would you tell me what prevents you from making a decision today?

Flowith: The Best Way to Handle Resistance

Flowith is a communication tool for neutralizing resistance while acknowledging a person's point of view. Once a Flowith statement has been used, it is usually followed by a question that leads the person toward an outcome that supports your original objective.

Use this technique to handle resistance from your employees, your boss, your customers, and even your children. You'll soon see how much more effective it is than simply disagreeing.

Flowith involves agreeing with the other person's statement in order to diffuse the resistance.

Caution: We often tell someone that we agree with them and then insert the word *but* before presenting our own point of view. *But,* however, negates everything that has been said before it. So eliminate that word from your Flowith vocabulary.

Follow these three simple steps:

1. Agree.

2. Insert the word "and."

3. Ask another question, one that supports your point of view and causes your partner to think constructively, along with you, for a solution.

Here are some examples:

Prospect: You just don't understand anything!

You: You're right, I don't. What specifically could I understand that we both could live with?

Or,

Prospect: You don't deliver on your promises.

You: You're right, we may have made some mistakes in the past. What can we do now to win back your trust?

Or:

Prospect: We just don't have the manpower to take on this project.

You: What you're saying makes sense. It's a big job. And how can we work together so we can get the job done?

Try the following examples yourself. It's a good idea to get someone else to help so you can "flow" each other.

Your people skills are terrible.

The price is too high.

Your competitor's product has more features.

You know, not every kid my age has to be in by 11!

The quality of your product is not the best.

You're just old fashioned.

You Don't Have to Be Sick to Get Better

As a sales doctor, your goal is to get the prospects emotionally involved in a search for the solution to their problems, issues, or concerns. Done properly, this also serves to create a sense of urgency and implies that you have a solution that they need to learn about.

In this way, the prospect is inclined to schedule your call, rather than leave you begging for an appointment. Remember, no begging anymore. Language like, "I'll give you a ring next Tuesday just to see if you're free," doesn't work. It sounds like selling, and it tells them you weren't doing anything anyway, so why not let you talk to them.

PRESCRIPTION FOR SUCCESS

As a sales doctor, your goal is to get the prospects emotionally involved in a search for the solution to their problems, issues, or concerns. Done properly, this also serves to create a sense of urgency and implies that you have a solution that they need to learn about.

The master sales professional understands that you can't really "sell" anything anyway. You must simply allow prospects to buy. So pay special attention to these next important steps, and you can set things up so that your prospects schedule your phone calls for you.

You: What is your biggest problem in sales/keeping track of information/your telecommunication system *(an area that gives you information regarding their use of your product or service)*? We generally find that organizations such as yours will at one time or another experience problems in the area of motivation and employee performance/obtaining new business and profitability/time management/inventory control *(three areas where your product or service helps solve problems)*. Can you help me?

Prospect: *(The prospect will tell you.)*

You: Can you help me further? Why did you pick that one? *(prying questions in order to get them to amplify their first answer)*

Or,

You: When you say . . ., what do you mean by that?

Or, (the best question in the world)

You: Oh? *(The prospect has no choice but to go on and tell you more.)*

If the prospect insists that nothing is wrong, say:

You: You mean everything is going well, and nothing is wrong?

If the resistance continues, say:

You: When you think about the last time you used (whatever your product or service is), are there any problems, issues, or concerns that come to mind?

Are there any areas in which you could use improvement? (Make a joke: You know you don't have to get sick to get better!)

Making It Hurt

It's very important once the prospects have identified a problem or area of concern to make them get emotionally involved in it so they want a cure.

If you went to the doctor for a routine check-up and she found something wrong, you'd suddenly feel sick. You might also, depending on the problem, be ready to do anything to find a cure. So play doctor!

You: What is this costing you in terms of reputation, time, or money? In round numbers? How much would that come to over, say, a year?

You: What have you done to fix this problem?

Prospect: (*They will tell you what they've tried.*)

You: And that's worked well for you?

You know it hasn't worked because they already said that they still have the problem. By asking them to remember and list all the things that they've done that haven't worked, you get them emotionally involved. They start to feel the pain and desperately want a solution.

You: This is all very interesting, but tell me this, are you committed to solving this problem?

Or,

You: Are you committed to correcting this situation in the future?

This is the big close. Once this question has been answered with an affirmative, you can be sure you are on your way to a sale.

If prospects say that they are interested rather than committed, suggest to them that you have learned over the years that the difference between interest and commitment is that interested people have no real need, a small budget, and are just beginning to shop. Those who have a commitment are willing to make decisions and take action to enhance, improve, or correct their company's performance, revenues, or productivity.

The following is a list of the ten best questions you can ask anytime:

1. That's a very good question. Can you help me? Why did you ask that?

2. Can you tell me why that's important to you?

3. Can you be more specific?

4. Can you tell me why?

5. When you say . . ., what do you mean by that? *(Insert any descriptive phrase or word your prospect uses, such as: "some difficulty," "top priority," "a lot," or "infrequently.")*

6. Oh? *(This forces them to expound on whatever they just said!)*

7. I'm not quite sure yet, can you help me?

8. Let's pretend that I said yes, or I said no—what difference would that make to you?

9. Which means?

10. You mean, you never have any problems, and things always go right? *(About the only time you ever want to use the words "never" and "always" in the sales process is when you're repeating them back to a prospect as a question.)*

The Sales Doctor® Qualifying Exam

1. What's your biggest problem in (insert your line of work)?

2. How long have you had it?

3. What have you done to fix it?

4. And that's worked well for you?

5. What is this costing you in terms of time, money, or reputation?

6. Do you have a budget set up to solve this problem?

7. Are you the person who makes these decisions?

8. Are you committed to finding a solution to this problem?

Chapter 8 Summary

1. Find the pain.

2. Qualify the prospect.

3. Make the presentation.

4. Never make the presentation until the first two steps have been accomplished.

5. Find the pain by asking open-ended questions.

PRESCRIPTION FOR SUCCESS

Do not offer solutions to problems that may not exist.
Do not answer questions that haven't been asked.

Keep the flow of information coming your way by *responding to a question with a question of your own,* and soften your question so it doesn't sound like a challenge.

Why?

✗ To discover the real question or problem

✗ To stay in control of the interview

✗ To avoid giving the wrong information

✗ To avoid falling into a black hole

Be gentle, precise, and when you meet with resistance, use the three steps of *Flowith:*

1. Agree.

2. Insert the word "and."

3. Ask another question from your point of view.

When you've found the pain, make sure the prospect is aware of being in pain and that the pain is out in the open now.

step 4: **budget, terms, and conditions**

Discovering the Budget

REMEMBER, a qualified prospect has three attributes:

1. A need, issue, or concern—which you've already established

2. A budget

3. The decision maker

Once you, as sales doctor, have uncovered the prospect's pain, you must establish whether they have "health insurance," so to speak. That is, do they have the budget to pay for your recommended treatment?

In Step 3, you've discovered the pain and through touching the sore spot, the prospect has become emotionally involved in obtaining a cure. Your objective now is to discuss budgets while that involvement is at a high point and the prospect is acutely aware of how much a cure is worth to them.

Prospects normally don't want to share their financial information with you, but it is important to discuss money up front, before you invest time and energy in a demo or presentation.

PRESCRIPTION FOR SUCCESS:

Don't make presentations to *unqualified* prospects. It wastes valuable time and money.

Review the problems the prospects have revealed and ask more questions, such as: "What kind of budget do you have for solving these problems?"

If they don't answer or don't want to share that with you, you probably have not established sufficient rapport or revealed enough "pain." Therefore, you might want to be a little more specific as you test the waters: "In another office like yours, it costs about $1,000 a month to deal with similar problems." Either of these methods gets the prospect's cards on the table. The response surely tells you whether you should continue your interview.

Sometimes, you get responses like, "Money is no object." When you hear this, you can bet on one of three things:

1. Money is no object because they don't have any.

2. You're not talking to the decision maker.

3. You are being shopped.

The following exchange illustrates how to graciously and delicately discover the budget.

You: And tell me, do you have a budget set aside to help fix this problem?

Prospect: Yes.

You: Would you mind sharing it with me?

Prospect: (They usually do mind.)

You: Can you tell me in round numbers, so I can know if we're in the same ballpark? *(Work them; they don't want to discuss "private" budgets.)*

Well, would you say it's more than $5,000 and less than $10,000?

Closer to $5,000 or closer to $10,000?

Keep narrowing it down and get as close as you can. At the very least, just establish that they have a budget. At that point, you can talk about it more as the process continues.

Prospect: I really have no idea. I've never done this before.

You: Okay. I understand that. Let's pretend it's the *(day of the job, end of the job, you just got the delivery, whatever)*. You have just been handed the bill. You look down to read it. What does it say? What do you see? *(Use neuro-linguistics. They usually have some idea.)*

Or,

Prospect: No, we don't have any budget or money.

You: Okay. And how were you hoping I could help you?

Or,

You: Have you set aside a budget for this product/service?

Prospect: How much does it cost?

You: Well, our solutions range from around $3,000 to $18,000. Would you say you are closer to $3,000 or to $18,000 in your ability to finance a solution to your problem?

Prospect: Closer to $3,000.

You: Can you tell me in round numbers how close?

Prospect: About $4,000.

If prospects say that they don't really have a budget right now, ask them to tell you when they will. If that approach doesn't elicit a timetable that you consider reasonable, it may be time to "go for no"—that is, *abort* the sales interview.

Never be afraid to go for no. If you aren't going to be able to put together a package that pleases both sides, you're better off finding that out in ten minutes rather than after you've wasted three hours.

Remember: *No* is the second-best answer you can get. The best, of course, is *yes.* But the answer you don't want, the one that is totally unacceptable, is, "I'll think it over, maybe" or "I'll get back to you."

That leaves both of you in limbo. Insist that the prospect decide between yes and no, with no being perfectly okay with you.

In order to finish qualifying your prospect and to reinforce what you are about to do, I have developed a technique that you can use.

Say to the prospect: "We've found that companies such as yours (or individuals like yourself) generally fall into one of four categories:

1. They are very interested in our product or service and they have a budget.

2. They are very interested in our product or service and they don't have a budget.

3. They have no interest in our product or service but they do have a budget.

4. They have no interest in our product or service and they don't have a budget.

"Can you help me? Which category would you say describes your situation?"

Depending on their response—whichever category they choose—you should ask the matching question:

1. What specifically were you hoping we could do for you?

2. What were you hoping we could do for you without any money?

3. Is there anything you would like to change or improve?

4. Why am I here?

If the prospects say they are in category one, they are *hot* prospects. If they are in categories two or three, they are *warm* or *cool*, depending on whether or not they are the decision makers. If they are in the fourth category, they are *cold* prospects and you shouldn't even be sitting with them.

If the prospects answer your exploratory comment about cost with, "That's a lot of money," you can respond with, "Oh. Can you help me? Relative to what?" and wait . . . .

Depending on their answer, you may have to ask them to suggest a number that they consider "workable."

If the figure they suggest is too low, it's up to you to maintain control and determine (1) if their figure represents an actual quote from another supplier and (2) whether you want to—or have to—either match the competition for strategic purposes or end the sales interview.

But beware: This shouldn't happen if you've established rapport and asked the kinds of questions that would reveal some pain. When you go to a doctor for a routine checkup and find out that, in fact, your life is in danger, you'll pay anything to be cured.

Put Your Cards on the Table

Along with the budget, you have to establish terms and conditions, such as credit applications, deposits, payments, payment plans, retainers, and time frame for implementation. It is important to discuss the available options up front so that both parties are prepared for what the other wants and is able to do.

If you come up against a problem when asking for a decision, don't back away in order to avoid rejection. Face it head on. Say, "We have a problem here." Let the prospects say, "What is it?" and work with you to establish a solution.

If they can't, it's time to say, "Well, then, it sounds as if our conversation is over." If they come back with, "Wait a minute . . . ," obviously their pain is intense, they need your cure, and whatever has been the sticking point between you and the prospect will get revealed and resolved.

If the prospects' answer reveals that you are too far apart to reach an agreement, this too could signal that it's time to go for no.

If the situation is clearly hopeless, you can still ask, "Before we hang up, off the record, what's the real reason you aren't going to be able to use our product (or service)?"

Listen carefully to the answer; you might learn something you can use next time. Or you may finally get the real reason, and then you can continue to sell.

Asking your prospects to qualify themselves is really the best way to establish an up-front contract. When you treat the specifics of the business transaction in an open and honest way, prospects tend to be more serious and honest with you. Most prospects respect business professionals who put their cards on the table from the beginning. So why wait?

Chapter 9 Summary

There are three requisites for qualifying a prospect:

1. Find a need.

2. Find a budget.

3. Find the decision maker.

Don't make presentations to unqualified prospects!
Don't be afraid to "go for no."
No is the second best answer you can get. It frees you to follow your recipe so you can get to the *yes* you want.

step 5: **finding the decision maker**

AFTER YOU DISCOVER the need and the budget, there is still one more requirement to qualify your prospect. You must make sure that you are talking to the person with the power to make the decision.

10	The After Sale
9	Close
8	Reinforcement
7	Presentation
6	Review
5	***Decision Maker***
4	Budget
3	Finding the Pain
2	Rapport
1	Pre-Call Planning

Many of today's sales professionals start by knowing very little about their prospects. They make calls to people who are at very low levels of management, and they usually remain with these non-decision-makers, with little or no success.

If you are at this level, it can be a very painful experience to graduate to the proper level in the decision-making hierarchy. You might find yourself stonewalled, blackballed, or even threatened. Attempting to go over your contact's head can result in being permanently banned from the company.

However, there are tools you can use to make sure you reach the proper contact at the beginning of your relationship with that "suspect," or potential prospect.

Most prospects say that they are the decision maker. It is important to qualify that without insulting them. In the area of decision-making policy, you have to determine who besides the person you're speaking with has to be involved in the decision, and how, when, and why they make their decisions.

With regard to committee or group decisions, you have to find out the names, titles, roles, and functions of each of the members and request to talk with each of them to conduct an interview.

In any business or organization, there is a chain of command. As sales professionals, your job is to start with the primary decision maker. If your research is done correctly, and you have found out who the chief corporate officer, CEO, owner, or head administrator is, your first and primary level of contact has already been located. *Always start at the top!*

PRESCRIPTION FOR SUCCESS:

When trying to discover the decision maker, start from the top down.

Eighty percent of the time, you will get the most knowledgeable person in the company on the line—the personal assistant to the top officer. That's the person you really want to interview and ask for help.

Your next step is to get the chief corporate officer to the phone. Before calling, you might use a mailing to introduce yourself and your product. A few days after your mailing, call the person for an interview. Use the mailing as your reason for calling.

You: Hi, I'm Chris Doe from the XYZ Company. I hope you had a chance to review the information I sent you recently. Oh, you have . . . that's great! I'm calling to arrange a mutually convenient time for me to phone so that we can share ideas concerning the information you received and to see how we can help each other.

What day are you looking at? *(No matter what the prospect says, respond with:)* I'm sorry, that's a bad day—I'm booked. Can you please pick another one? Good. What time? Can we make that at 3:10? *(Or 10:40; you'll look busy if you pick a time that's off the o'clock.)*

At this point in the selling cycle, one of three scenarios will occur: Either the chief operating officer will talk to you, you'll be introduced to someone else, or, for whatever reason, you will not be able to go any further. If you are dead-ended, just go on to other prospects.

If the chief officer will talk with you, one of two situations will result from your conversation. You will either deal entirely with the primary officer, or the primary officer will want to introduce you to someone else after your initial presentation. If the chief officer is the one you will deal with throughout the selling cycle, just continue your sales approach.

However, if the primary contact wants to introduce you to someone else after your initial phone call, let the person do so.

Remember: It is better to be "passed down" the corporate ladder than to be "passed up" the hierarchy.

Ask the chief officer to introduce you personally. That gives you more credibility at the next level of contact. If the CEO does not personally introduce you to the next level of contact, simply make it clear that you are calling at the CEO's suggestion.

Make sure you let the CEO know that you will keep their office informed about all future developments and make sure to let the new contact know that the CEO is aware of what's happening.

Again, your new contact will either continue with you directly or, in turn, introduce you to someone else.

You: I realize you will make the final decision, and the president approves your decision. But if you do not get involved in the presentation and evaluation, could you introduce me to the correct person?

Your job is to determine who gives final approval and who has the authority to authorize the purchase or placement. Once you have done that, get those people working with you. When you are introduced to each new person, make sure you maintain contact with the other levels. Leave the channel of communication open all the way up to the CEO.

If you start at the bottom with a purchasing agent, you will find that it is much more difficult to be introduced up the corporate ladder than down.

Who's Who in Decision-Making?

Let's identify the typical levels of contact and their usual basic functions and corresponding decision-making authority.

PURCHASING/OFFICE SERVICES

The purchasing/office services personnel are usually concerned with hardware, costs, machine specifications, and maintaining the status quo. Unless higher level management complains about a piece of equipment, their attitude is usually "don't make waves." Depending on the company, these individuals usually do not have a wide range of authority.

MIDDLE MANAGEMENT

Middle management is usually responsible for developing and implementing programs to fulfill the corporate goals and objectives. Their level of authority is usually higher than the individuals in the previous category. They could be input sources who may or may not influence the final decision, depending on the organization.

SENIOR MANAGEMENT

Senior management personnel are usually concerned with the big picture. They determine the corporate goals and objectives and have fiscal accountability. They usually have to answer to stockholders or taxpayers. This is the level of contact that successful salespeople are primarily concerned with in their everyday sales efforts.

In most cases, senior management prefers a systematic and organized approach to managing their operations. For example, many companies have programs with other companies that provide them with discounts for multiple purchases. This gives them value for their money and provides them with quality products at lower cost.

This may be something you can offer a new client or customer. Remember: When an account has already accepted the concept associated with your program or product, most of your selling obstacles are behind you. A purchasing agent will not think along these lines.

Senior management is also concerned with factors like inflation, operation costs, productivity, and energy conservation. In commercial major accounts, these factors affect the bottom line. In government accounts, controlling these costs ensures the best value possible for every tax dollar spent.

People at this level are also concerned with long-range results and growth. They have to plan for systems and programs that assist them in getting to where they want to go. If you can fit in with their plans, you could grow with them.

They want to know better ways to manage their business. It's your responsibility to identify a better way. Purchasing agents do not look for a change unless senior management asks them to. Remember: Although senior management is concerned with a good return on their investment, this does not necessarily mean the lowest price.

Examples of Contact Levels for Senior Management

Medical

Resident Chief Physicians
Hospital Administrators
Lab Technicians
Pathologists
Purchasing Managers

Commercial
Chairperson of the Board
President
Executive Vice President
Vice President for Administration
Vice President for Finance
Divisional Vice President

Government, City
Mayor
City Manager
Assistant to Mayor

Government, County
County Commissioners
County Managers

Government, State
Governor
Lieutenant Governor
Comptroller
Agency Heads
Department Secretary

Government, Federal—Civilian
Department Heads
Agency Directors

Government, Federal—Military
Commanding Officers
Executive Officers

Education District
Superintendent
Curriculum Director

Assistant Superintendent
Business Manager

Colleges/Universities
Chancellor
Provost
Vice Provost
President
Vice President
Dean
Department Head

More Tips for Pinpointing the Decision Maker

Of course, you'll need some soft language to help you weed out the real decision makers from the self-appointed ones after you find out their budget:

You: Let's assume that I can offer you a solution to this problem at a price we can agree on. Would you be the person who makes these decisions?

Prospect: Yes.

You: Does that mean that you don't need anyone else's approval?

Prospect: Yes.

Or,

Prospect: No. There's a board that I have to present a proposal to, and the members make the ultimate decision.

You: Would it be helpful at some point for me to talk with the members of the board with you to present the *(program, idea, product)* more fully?

Or,

Prospect: No. Those decisions are made by *(so and so)*.

You: Great, can you help set something up for me? *(If no:)* Well, can you help me get in touch with *(so and so)*? May I use your name when I speak to them? *(Again, always try to turn the call into a referred lead.)*

This is the time to eliminate "think it overs" and "maybes." You are asking the prospect for a decision to make a decision. "I'll think it over" is a decision *not* to make a decision. It is also a nice way of saying no without actually saying no. This kind of response leaves you hanging on to false hopes.

You: Assuming that we can deliver a solution that satisfies *(list the pains)*, and if we can do that within your budget, when do you see a more reliable *(or faster, or easier)* system in use here?

Prospect: Well, as soon as possible.

You: Fine. Are you able to make the yes or no decision regarding this *(product or service)*, or will you need to talk it over with anyone else in your organization?

Prospect: I may talk it over with my office manager, but I make the final decision.

You: Will you be able to make a yes or no decision at the time of the demonstration, with no being perfectly okay?

Prospect: Yes.

Or,

You: Will you be able to make a yes or no decision at the time of the presentation, with no being perfectly okay?

Prospect: No.

You: Would you be willing to tell me why?

Prospect: Yes. I have to shop around. I have three other vendors to see before I make a decision.

You: I see. Could I ask you a hypothetical question?

Prospect: Sure.

You: Let's pretend for a minute that you like our system so much that you decide after seeing it that you don't want to use your precious time looking at others. What would I have to have to show you so that you could make that kind of time-saving decision?

Take notes, folks. They're telling you what you need to do to sell them at the presentation. Or,

You: Will you be able to make a yes or no decision at the time of my presentation, with no being perfectly okay?

Prospect: No.

You: Would you be willing to tell me why?

Prospect: Yes. I have to shop around. I have three other vendors to see before I make a decision.

You: Oh. I see. Could I ask you a question off the record? What would it really take for us to do business?

Again, listen carefully. By taking them "off the record," they have an opportunity to open up.

Chapter 10 Summary

1. When trying to discover the decision maker, start from the top of the organization and work down.

2. Keep track of everyone you talk to and find out where they fit into the picture.

3. Be sure to get introductions whenever possible.

4. Keep each person you've been introduced to up-to-date on your progress.

5. If you have developed a special rapport with someone inside a company, try to enlist that person as a guide. An inside "shepherd" can not only help you find your way but also tell you how others are reacting to your approaches.

step 6: **the review**

YOU HAVE NOW reached the end of the first part of the direct sales process. It is time to review what has transpired so far.

10	The After Sale
9	Close
8	Reinforcement
7	Presentation
6	***Review***
5	Decision Maker
4	Budget
3	Finding the Pain
2	Rapport
1	Pre-Call Planning

Review Tip #1

Make sure you have rapport with the prospect. Having rapport means that you have established credibility and trust and that the prospect is now comfortable enough with you to answer your questions truthfully. You can then discover some pain by probing further about the issues.

Review Tip #2

You've established or uncovered a budget or ballpark budget, you're talking to the decision maker and that person's relevant advisers, you know who the competition is, and you've established a second appointment for the prospect to review your transaction and to make decisions.

Review Tip #3

Go over your notes with the prospect. Come to an agreement about what happened during that day's transaction and what will happen the next time you talk. Say to the prospect something like:

> Today, we decided that you have the following problems, issues, or concerns *(list them; you should have at least five)*. When you've tested the samples and we talk next week, I'll show you how we can help solve these problems within the budget you've given me. Then, can you agree to make a decision as to whether or not you want to go ahead with our product or service, with "no" being perfectly okay? Does that sound fair to you?

Get them to agree to make a decision after your next conversation, with no being perfectly okay. If they must submit your proposal to a board or committee after they see it, try to get an appointment to talk to the board members yourself. Keep in mind that a board is a group of individuals; they have to be sold as individuals—*one at a time.*

PRESCRIPTION FOR SUCCESS

Make sure you don't end your interview without making an appointment for a second interview. This saves the time and energy of playing phone tag later.

If they have to see your presentation alone first, get them to agree that they will at least make a decision as to whether or not they will submit your product or service to the board at the next opportunity. This agreement is called an *up-front contract.*

Make sure you don't end your interview without making an appointment for a second interview. Before you hang up, get your calendar out to save the time and energy of playing phone tag later.

The Second Interview

With your prospect, review your up-front contract from the first interview, paying special attention to rapport. Say to the prospect:

> Last week, we agreed that if I can show you how we can solve the problems you listed to your satisfaction, and at a price within your budget, that you would make a yes or no decision today, with no being perfectly okay. Is that a fair statement?

Then review the problems and ask them if those are all the problems they have. Read the list carefully. Remember: You should have five problems. If you don't have five, the close may not be so powerful, as you'll see in Chapter 14.

Chapter 11 Summary

1. Make sure you have rapport with the prospect.

2. Make sure that you've established or uncovered a budget or ballpark budget, that you're talking to both the decision maker and relevant advisers, that you know who the competition is, and that you've established a second appointment for the prospect to review your transaction and to make decisions.

3. Go over your notes with the prospect. Come to an agreement about what happened during that day's transaction and what will happen the next time you talk.

4. Then get the prospect to agree to at least make a decision as to whether or not to submit your product or service to the board at the next opportunity. This is your *up-front contract.*

5. Make sure you don't end your interview without making an appointment for a second interview. Before you hang up, get your calendar out to save the time and energy of playing phone tag later.

step 7: **the presentation**

IF STEPS 1 through 6 of the sales interview process have been thoroughly completed, then this step will flow easily, with the prospect participating actively in your presentation. If done correctly, this will be an interactive process. Your prospect must be involved at this stage.

This is not the time to be lecturing to a silent audience.

You have, ideally, listed five, or at least a minimum of three, of your prospect's problems.

Now, ask the prospect to choose the most important problem for you to solve first. Go over exactly how you are going to solve this problem and ask if the prospect agrees that the problem would now be eliminated.

Do not go on until the prospect is satisfied. As you attempt to eliminate each of the prospect's problems, make sure you ask if each is solved 100 percent. If not, review the problem and your solution again until you get to 100 percent. Then cross the problem off the prospect's list.

PRESCRIPTION FOR SUCCESS

Warning: Never, *ever* begin a sales interview with your presentation.

Resolve two out of three, or three out of the five problems you have listed. Make sure *you don't do* a complete presentation. After you reach that point, begin your reinforcement, which is where prospects close themselves on your product or service, and you facilitate that process with the appropriate additional information (see Step 8).

During the presentation, *primary videos* are going to need to picture your presentation, *primary audios* are going to need to hear and talk, and *primary kinos* are going to need to sense and feel touched by your presentation.

Using a sample test kit as an example, *videos* pay more attention to the look of the kit, the brochures, and material they can see. *Audios* are more impressed by the sound of the materials it's made from—if they are solid, well made, and fit together well. They likely would like to hear testimonials. They are impressed by what other people and the experts have to say about the kit. *Kinos* need a hands-on experience. They need to use the kit, explore the feel of it.

Again, don't let your success at any stage of your presentation lead you to think it's time to make a pitch for something that hasn't been discussed before. Only address the needs that your prospect has told you about and that you have both agreed to deal with.

Chapter 12 Summary

1. You should not be lecturing to a silent audience.

2. After having listed three to five of your prospect's problems, ask the prospect to choose the most important problem for you to solve first.

3. Do not go on to the next problem until the prospect is satisfied.

4. Be sure to resolve two out of three, or three out of the five problems you have listed.

5. Whatever you do, don't complete the presentation!

Remember: During the presentation, *primary videos* need to picture your presentation, *primary audios* need to hear and talk, and *primary kinos* need to sense and feel touched by your presentation.

step 8: the reinforcement

AT THIS STAGE, it is important to know where you stand. Take the prospect's temperature. After solving three of the problems 100 percent, say to the prospect:

You: We've addressed some of the issues that are important to you. I know we have other issues to discuss, but to get an idea of where we're at in the process, can you help me? On a scale from 0 to 10, with 0 being that you are not at all interested in our product or service and 10 being that you can already see it as a valuable addition to your business, where are we now?

To make this question more powerful, use your knowledge of neuro-linguistics to customize the question for the prospect.

If the prospect is a *primary video*, ask, "Where do you see us?"

If the prospect is a *primary audio*, ask, ""Where would you say we are?"

If the prospect is a *primary kino*, ask, "Where do you feel we are at this moment?"

If the prospect is at a 6 or above, ask what you need to do to get to a 10. If you can satisfy the prospect's request, do it and take their temperature again.

If the prospect is at 5 or below, you have an emergency. It means that you did not fully qualify and uncover the pain. Say:

You: With such a low number, can you help me? What did I say or do wrong during my presentation to receive such a low number? What do we need to go over that I misunderstood or left out, before we can go forward?

Continue to question and probe until you discover what went wrong, so that you can correct it.

If the prospect has not reached 10 before you finish demonstrating, you must finish the demonstration and proceed to the summary.

Summarize the pains that have been relieved and the buying criteria that have been satisfied, gaining the prospect's agreement as you go. Once you have completed the summary, ask if there are any questions. If there are, probe and question to ascertain what it is specifically that would be needed to be done to get to 10.

When the prospect reaches 10, stop! Again, the prospect has "self-closed." *Do not solve* the other problems. In layperson's terms, to go any farther is called talking yourself out of a sale. Instead, ask the prospect, "What would you like me to do now?"

When this step has been completed, it is finally time for the close.

Chapter 13 Summary

1. Here in the reinforcement step is where you take the prospect's temperature.

2. After solving three of the prospect's problems, ask the prospect to evaluate things on a scale from 0 to 10, that is from no interest to fully satisfied.

3. Be sure to customize your question using your prospect's primary representational system.

step 9: **the close**

CLOSING THE SALE is the end result of all your previous work. If you have properly qualified and uncovered the pain, correctly discovered the budget, established the decision to be made and who makes it, and proved yourself and your product in the presentation, the close is easy.

10	The After Sale
9	***Close***
8	Reinforcement
7	Presentation
6	Review
5	Decision Maker
4	Budget
3	Finding the Pain
2	Rapport
1	Pre-Call Planning

Because you take the prospect's temperature during the presentation, you will know when to close—when you get to 10.

After you solve the fourth problem, ask the prospect where she or he is now. Then ask again what the prospect would like to do. The usual response is to solve the last problem. At this point, the prospect knows what is happening and usually enjoys taking part in the close.

When you get to 10, you must ask, "What do we need to do now with regard to the order—or purchase order—and delivery?"

Although the sale isn't closed until you get to 10, your prospect may give you a buying signal along the way. A buying signal can be defined as a verbal or audible sign that indicates that the prospect is starting to see, hear, or feel himself owning or using your product or service.

However, a buying signal is not necessarily a sign that the prospect is ready to close, so don't jump the gun. Stick to your plan. A buying signal is really an opportunity for you to cement the value of your product or service. You can accomplish this by having the prospect talk about the experience of using your product or service.

Here are some buying signals and the appropriate responses:

Prospect: That's fantastic!

You: What's the most fantastic thing about it?

Or,

Prospect: I really like that feature.

You: What specifically is it that you like?

Or,

Prospect: When could I have delivery?

You: When would you prefer delivery?

Or,

Prospect: What about follow-up service?

You: Good question. What specific area would you like me to address?

Physical buying signals might include the following:

✗ The prospect has a "smile" in his or her voice.

✗ The prospect suddenly becomes friendlier.

✗ The prospect suddenly relaxes.

✗ The prospect takes a deep breath.

✗ The prospect discusses ordering details.

✗ The prospect makes numerical calculations.

When you question a buying signal, you help prospects to close themselves. While answering your question, the prospect is further convincing herself of the value of the specific feature and of your product in general.

PRESCRIPTION FOR SUCCESS

If you can remember to match and mirror your prospect's words, tone, and physiology when questioning the prospect, you will be building your close with even more powerful tools.

Even at this point, you don't want to break rapport by asking for an order prematurely. Continue mirroring and decide if this is the correct time to take the prospect's temperature. Or try something like this, "Off the record, how does it look/sound/feel so far?"

The minute you get the prospect to say you're at 10, stop! Don't make the mistake of overselling. When the prospect says he is at 10, that prospect is sold.

Gently remind the prospect of the agreement to make a yes or no decision. Ask for that decision and be quiet. Do not say a word! Wait for the prospect to decide, even if the silence feels very uncomfortable. You are in control.

At this point, if you are dealing with someone who still has to get a board or committee approval, get the person to allow you to present your product or service or talk to the board committee yourself—one by one. Convince them that you can best represent the product. If the prospect denies this request, ask if the prospect would feel confident enough about your product or service to answer any questions the board posed. If not, *coach the prospect* to present for you.

Remember—there are no magic closes. No telemarketer can rescue a mishandled sale. The sales professional earns a close by establishing the nature of the prospect's pain, the budget, and the decision-making ability. The professional then convincingly demonstrates how the product or service can remove that pain and eliminate the problem.

The emotional buying decision is made when prospects feel that the purchase of the product or service will satisfy their needs and alleviate their pain.

A thorough qualification of the prospect is vital to a successful close. Closing begins with your first contact with the prospect. Your interest in your prospect's needs and your ability to listen create a positive image for yourself, your company, and your product.

Chapter 14 Summary

Remember: Closing the sale is the end result of all your previous work. If you have properly qualified and uncovered the pain, correctly discovered the budget, established the decision to be made and who makes it, and proved yourself and your product in the presentation, the close is easy.

Tip: After you solve the fourth problem, ask the prospects where they are now. Then ask them again what they would like to do. They usually say to solve the last problem. At this point, the prospects know what is happening, and they usually enjoy taking part in their own close.

15

step 10: **after the sale**

AFTER YOU HAVE entered the order for your prospects and repeated it back to them for confirmation, ask them if they know what the order represents.

They usually respond by saying that it's a contract.

"Yes," you say, "and it's the beginning of our relationship and my commitment to work with you. Are you okay with that?"

10	***The After Sale***
9	Close
8	Reinforcement
7	Presentation
6	Review
5	Decision Maker
4	Budget
3	Finding the Pain
2	Rapport
1	Pre-Call Planning

If they're not, review whatever elements they are uncomfortable with.

If they are comfortable, then you have just reinforced the sale and started to create a feeling of loyalty and trust with your new clients.

The follow-up and follow-through calls that you make to your customers are proof of your commitment to an ongoing relationship with them. Don't make the mistake of waiting until there's a problem to talk to them again. Call and say, "I wanted to make sure that our delivery was prompt and that the right material came and there were no problems."

PRESCRIPTION FOR SUCCESS:

Become a resource that your clients will use and appreciate. Understand the difference between serving your clients and merely servicing them.

These calls also serve your after-market and referral business. No one wants to start the selling cycle all over again, time after time. Yet many sales professionals operate in this fashion and end up working much harder than they need to.

Eighty percent of your business comes from 20 percent of your clients and introductions. Every time you make a sale, ask for a referral. Write the name on a 3-by-5 index card, along with the name of the customer who gave it to you. Get as much information as you can about the new prospect from your customer.

Each time you make a sale from a referral, be sure to write a thank you note to the customer who gave you the lead. Make sure the note is handwritten on a card, not typed on a letterhead.

Always remember the value of your clients. Treat them like gold and they will give you gold. Successful business in the twenty-first century is about people sticking together, caring, and sharing. Every client, no matter how small, is a valuable one. Being a master sales professional is a never-ending process of good communication, patience, and reinforcement.

Enjoy the business and lifestyle you have created. If nurtured and cared for properly, it will bring you wealth, fulfillment, freedom, and happiness.

And be proud of yourself. You have taken the first steps to realizing your dreams. The hardest part of anything is to begin it, so you are already on your way.

Review Questions for the 10-Step Interview

Challenge yourself by answering the following questions regarding the ten chapters in Part 2. If you need help with any of the answers, just turn back and reread the section or sections that require review. Certainly the better you know this material, the more successful you will be when conducting your own sales interviews.

1. What are the three things you need to know in order to qualify a prospect?

2. What should you do each time you talk to a prospect?

3. What are the three main sensory channels people use when communicating?

4. List three things you should mirror during a sales call.

5. As a "sales doctor," what is the first step you need to take?

6. Reverse the following: "Is your product very expensive?"

7. Explain the three steps of *Flowith* and give an example.

8. What are the three attributes of a qualified prospect?

9. What does "money is no object" really mean?

10. Which level of management should you approach about your product or service?

11. How can you turn being introduced down a corporate chain into a referred lead?

12. Describe an up-front contract.

13. How many problems should be on your review list?

14. What should you do if a prospect refuses to go any further?

15. How does neuro-linguistics help you during your presentation?

16. How can you make sure that the presentation flows easily?

17. What should you do if a problem is not solved to your prospect's satisfaction?

18. When does closing begin?

19. Does a buying signal indicate that the prospect is ready to be closed?

20. What is the right time to close?

21. What should you do every time you make a sale?

22. What is the "rule of three"?

23. Define "rapport."

24. What is the purpose of reversing?

25. What technique can you use for finding out a prospect's budget?

26. How do you deal with a decision-making committee or board?

27. List as many words and phrases you can think of that are used by each primary sensory type. (Try and think of some that are not listed in this book and keep an open list near your phone.)

PART THREE
Staying on Top

why sales careers plateau

GENERALLY SPEAKING, careers don't burn out—*people burn out!* And if you're finding yourself unmotivated or depressed because of a so-called plateaued sales career, look again . . . the plateau may be something going on within yourself.

Reason #1 for Why Careers Burn Out: Resistance to Change

It's no secret: Business is rapidly changing, and as a twenty-first century sales professional, you are faced with more decisions than ever before. In fact, during your lifetime, you will face ten or fifteen major change-related decisions, many having to do with your career, and another twenty-five to thirty of stress-inducing proportions. Developing strategies for dealing with change is one of the most important steps in fighting plateaus in a professional selling career.

HOW TO DEAL WITH CHANGE

There are three ways people and organizations change:

> *Shock: 60 percent of change*—They react to a trigger event that is sudden and painful, such as a sickness or a downsizing, which creates a physical, emotional, and/or psychological response. These are the *reactives*, and this is how most people and companies change.

> *Evolution: 20 percent of change*—The person or organization doesn't do anything. They put off and procrastinate so that when change occurs, any possible response is more often than not too little too late.

> *Choice: 20 percent of change*—This is where you want to be—with the people and organizations that regularly plan a course for the future. They make proactive, ongoing changes and are on time with them. An adjustable and flexible person or company thrives in a rapidly changing environment.

THE FOUR RULES OF EFFECTIVE CHANGE

Rule #1: No one can change you, and you can't change anyone else. You must admit your need, stop denying your problem, and accept responsibility for changing yourself.

Rule #2: Habits aren't broken, but rather are replaced by layering new behavior patterns on top of the old ones. This process usually takes at least a year. Some motivational speakers assert that a person can learn a new habit in twenty-one days. I disagree. It can take you that long just to learn the motions of a new skill.

Don't expect immediate results from whatever program you install in your company, your institution, or your home. Give it a year and stick with it, knowing that your new way can last a lifetime.

Rule #3: A daily routine adhered to over time will become second nature, like riding a bicycle. If you want to be successful, begin acting successful in the company of successful people.

Rule #4: Having changed a habit, stay away from the old, destructive environment. To remain successful in business, you must be on a team in which each member takes responsibility for being a leader. If you leave the team environment, you must not return to the cynical, pre-knowledge-era company ways.

Reason #2 for Why Careers Burn Out: Relying Too Much on Your Own Wisdom

No matter how intelligent a company president may be—that officer still relies on a group of people (otherwise known as a *board of directors*) to steer the company in the most advantageous, profitable directions. So what does this have to do with your successful sales career? Well, just as most large companies acknowledge the importance of a qualified board of directors, many successful sales professionals have opted for their own personal board of directors to steer their careers in the most advantageous and profitable directions as well.

Think of a personal board as your "inner circle"; each person on your board shares in the most important information about your personal and professional life. Consider carefully every individual you invite to be on your board. The aim should be to find people who can remain on your board for the rest of your life. Of course, you can always make changes to the people on your board, but a real richness comes from working together during good times and bad. Like a great bottle of wine, proper "aging" of your board gives it fullness, maturity, and increasing value.

GETTING STARTED: DEVELOPING YOUR PERSONAL BOARD OF DIRECTORS

Let's start with the obvious. Your personal board of directors might include a doctor as a health/medical resource, a CPA for tax advice, an attorney for legal guidance, a banker for financial guidance, and a religious leader for spiritual support. Here are some of the less obvious: a sales and marketing professional, a public relations expert, a business coach, a child care specialist, a human resource professional, a Webmaster for Internet guidance, and an executive in a dissimilar industry and/or a business owner in your same industry—but not a competitor.

WORKING WITH YOUR BOARD

Once you have formed your personal board of directors, the next step is to make a list of the ways your board can assist and support your success. Some examples of professional and personal topics to discuss with your board are a new career, the start of a new business, advancement in your current company, the relocation of your family for professional or personal reasons, how to handle a problem employee or supplier, life and legacy planning, your children and their development, financial planning, and the health of your marriage. You see, your board members will be a rich resource to you in many ways, as long as you speak openly and truthfully with them and are open to their specific advice and feedback.

PRESCRIPTION FOR SUCCESS
Remember: Perfect practice makes perfect decisions.

Success Tip: While your board can give you powerful guidance and suggestions, the final decision must always be yours. When making an important professional or personal decision, take a blank sheet of paper and list all the pros and cons surrounding the issue. Then ask for and gather the feedback from your board. Next, write a brief summary statement to yourself explaining the reasons for your decision and store this sheet in a special place. Finally, mark your calendar for some point in the future to evaluate the results of this important decision. A review of each important decision you make during your lifetime helps you evaluate your accuracy and clarity about the future. Remember: Perfect practice makes perfect decisions.

COMMUNICATING WITH YOUR BOARD

The next step is to decide how often to meet with your board. For some, monthly is perfect; for others, twice a year is great; and many meet on a quarterly basis. The frequency is up to you and your board members, but the frequency should depend on the velocity of issues or decisions you are making. Here are some examples of ways you can meet or communicate with your board: in person, by telephone, teleconference as a group, e-mail, fax, letter, video conferencing, or during a nice meal. With today's wide range of technology, the distance between you and your board members is no longer an issue. Instead, invite only the best to be on your board and allow technology to facilitate your communications.

Success Tip: As you invite each member to participate on your board, be very clear about your expectations for each board member, the frequency with which you should meet or be in touch, and your need for pointed and honest feedback. After each person agrees to be on your board, discuss how they would like to be compensated for their time. In most cases, a trade or barter is done for goods or services. In many cases, a small gift or favor is enough. If necessary, offer to pay a small fee to each board member, as the value of their feedback will be returned many times over.

Techniques for Jumpstarting a Comeback—Personal

Seek and share ideas. Seek information regularly on different topics—in journals, magazines, the Net, and associations. Share those ideas with your colleagues and your customers.

Build your confidence, credibility, and knowledge to make more sales.

Share success. Create opportunities to share news of your successes with others—not only big, noteworthy successes but also the smaller ones that add up to big wins. Build a confidence and support network by telling others of that great cold call, the super game of catch with your child, or any success you experience.

Use creative relaxation. Sit comfortably, eyes closed. Breathe deeply. Visualize a pleasing, relaxing place. As thoughts enter your mind, let them come and go. Concentrate on your visual place. Enjoy ten to fifteen minutes visualizing that place ("being there"). You should do this frequently, at least once a day.

Be a maestro. Arms straight out at your sides (like a T), bend your arms at the elbow, letting your lower arms hang down freely. Now, with exaggerated movement, swing your lower arms back and forth vigorously, as if you are leading an orchestra. Create energy as you expend it. Breathe deeply. Go for one to three minutes. (This is a great energizer during a string of cold calls.)

Smile (and laugh) at least twenty-five times day. Count each time until the smiling becomes a habit. . . . Then you won't need to count. Soon you'll be at twenty-five before 10 a.m.

19 Quick Techniques for Reigniting a Plateaued Sales Career—Professional

You don't have to wait for your new habits to take effect to start seeing results. Try doing some of the things on the following list.

1. Ask for new assignments.

2. Assign yourself to special task forces or focus groups.

3. Challenge yourself with new products.

4. Ask to participate in ad hoc problem-solving sessions on major concerns.

5. "Profile" and become a company expert on a certain class of trade or industry.

6. Set higher goals for yourself with realistic time frames.

7. Participate vigorously in every sales contest your company offers.

8. Ask for additional training in sales areas.

9. Attend every sales seminar your company offers.

10. Read a minimum of one sales book each month.

11. Listen to audio (motivational, professional) seminars on your way to the office.

12. Study journals and newsletters pertaining to your industry.

13. Volunteer to help train new sales representatives.

14. Get more involved in planning your own career goals and ways to achieve them.

15. Work with a professional career counselor.

16. Join local professional or trade organizations.

17. Attend outside conferences that relate to your industry.

18. Ask to be sent on a college recruitment visit.

19. Try role-playing over the phone.

Chapter 16 Summary

Careers don't burn out; it's the person. If you find yourself unmotivated or depressed because of a stalled sales career, consider that the cause could be from within. Learn and apply strategies for getting back on track:

1. Learn how to deal with change. No one can change you, and you can't change anyone else. You must admit your need,

stop denying your problem, and accept responsibility for changing yourself.

2. Create your own board of directors. Think of this personal board as your "inner circle," consisting of people who share in the very important information about your personal and professional life.

optimize your time with client categories

Platinum Clients

WHO ARE THE top 4 percent of your revenue producers? These are your *platinum* clients. As you plan your client calls, these clients must be contacted every month. On the one hand, one of the quickest ways to lose business is to take it for granted. From another perspective, if these businesses are already contributing to your success, does it not seem logical that you would want to build on this relationship? Be sure you are meeting all their needs. Platinum clients are unconditional givers. Take very good care of them and let them take care of you too. You want to be certain that there is no reason for a competitor to begin nibbling away at your good work.

Gold Clients

The top 20 percent of your revenue producers are your *gold* clients. There is room to grow in your business with them. As you plan your time and prepare your marketing strategies, be certain to contact your gold clients monthly. They are "sold" on you and your business. Furthermore, 20 percent of your gold clients are willing—*if you ask them*—to work for you in offering leads and recommending new clients for your business. These gold clients are your most valuable resources. Treat them with care and attention, and they will be instrumental in helping you grow your business. You must acknowledge and recognize them on a consistent basis. In some circles, they are also known as "golden geese." Don't kill them to get their eggs.

Success Tip: As you plan your time and prepare your marketing strategies, be certain to include contact with your gold clients and platinum clients monthly—*at a minimum.* Pay attention to changes in their markets. Watch carefully for signs and opportunities. And be ready to anticipate their needs. You are not an order taker! You are providing a valuable service to their business, and monthly contact is important to the growth of these valuable relationships.

Silver "At-Leaster" Clients

As the middle 60 percent, your *silver* clients bring in 15 percent of your business. The best way to avoid attracting "at-leaster" clients is for you to avoid becoming an "at-leaster" sales professional yourself. In fact, struggling, bottom-feeder salespeople never attract top-level clients, no matter how hard they work.

AVOIDING THE AT-LEASTER PHENOMENON

If you've ever watched the opening of ABC's *Wide World of Sports*, then you've seen the winning runner break through the finish line, arms upraised in triumph, elated by the "thrill of victory." Of course, you've also seen the championship skier as he miscalculates and goes tumbling down the slopes into the "agony of defeat."

Victory and defeat. Winning and losing. Good and bad. All are similar concepts, right? The thing is, both these athletes are winners. Why? *Because only winners enter the race in the first place.*

Whether it's business, professional life, athletics—or even love—only those who are ready to risk losing, willing to accept the consequences, and able to *profit* from their losses ever know the taste of victory.

The risk involved in becoming a winner is a tall order for a salesperson, and the reason so many sales forces are suffering isn't because they lack winners on their teams, but because too many of their players won't enter the race. While the thrill of victory is undeniably seductive, the agony of defeat is often more intimidating.

Just what makes the fear of losing so immobilizing? The reasons are buried in our social conscience, where attitudes we hardly understand and barely acknowledge shape our thinking and actions. Perhaps the most powerful mixed message we receive as children is the belief we hold about winning and losing. "It's not whether you win or lose, it's how you play the game," we learn. But what we really believe is the dictum of football coach Vince Lombardi: "Winning isn't everything—it's the only thing." Is it any wonder, then, that most people would rather forgo the thrill of victory than risk the agony of defeat?

THE COMFORT ZONE

Most people tend to be non-risktakers. Their tombstones could easily read: "Died at 30 . . . buried at 80." They're men and women who've settled at an early age into the comfort zone of mediocrity. As justification for the grayness of their lives, they tell themselves: "Well, I may not have won, but *at least I didn't lose.*"

In years of working with sales organizations, I've found that 60 percent of the nation's sales force is made up of at-leasters. Stymied by their fears, hung up between failure and world-class success, occasionally actualizing their potential (but sure to fall back), at-leasters—with their seesaw sales performance records—are a mysterious drain on their companies' sales records, representing a major hidden loss and often infecting the entire corporation with the at-leaster virus.

The profession of selling, more than almost any other profession, is judged on *measurable results*, which makes sales professionals particularly susceptible to at-leasterism. For managers, the challenge becomes one of how to revitalize this group—to turn those mushy "50 percenters" into true winners.

In their attempt to put solid ground under their psyches, salespeople define themselves in one of three ways, all based on measurable results. They're either winners, losers, or something in between. How they see themselves—this internal picture—becomes the face that looks back at them in the corporate washroom mirror.

"Loser" salespeople see themselves inescapably hedged in by their limitations. Lifelong low self-esteem chronically inhibits their sales ability. They blame themselves when something goes wrong, unable to examine the circumstances or analyze the situation. Loser salespeople occupy 20 percent of the sales jobs in this country, but since they almost never make quota, they eventually get turned out, making room for a new crop of underachievers.

At the same time, the infamous 80/20 rule tells us that 20 percent of the sales force is making 80 percent of the sales. This 20 percent is naturally made up of winner salespeople. Despite the fact that we may all be born winners, after a good dose of mixed messages, eroded confidence, daily pessimism, and fear of failure, most "born winners" metamorphose into something else. Those who do survive are the ones who've developed the tools they need to keep their high-esteem intact. Winners see themselves as winners and deliver like pros—even when they fail, lose, and lose again. They're self-motivated, they believe in themselves, and they know they make a difference. In major league baseball, the leading home-run hitter often leads the league in strikeouts as well, but that doesn't keep him from going up to the plate and taking a healthy swing.

Winners also take full responsibility for what went wrong; they just don't blame themselves. They feel good no matter how they perform on any one day or in any one role. Winners know you can't win if you're afraid to lose, and that's where they differ from the at-leasters.

At-leasters look in the mirror and see confusion. They define a string of successes as a run of luck. When they do extremely well (for instance, closing 10 for 10 on a given day), at-leasters worry they really aren't as good as they may appear. Initial elation quickly gives way to secret fears: exposure, expectation, inability to repeat their success, and, ultimately, failure. They quickly retreat back into that gray area of mediocrity, where they hug their lucky win and say: *"At least* I didn't lose."

And when at-leasters strike out, they deny responsibility for their failures. "It wasn't my fault in the first place," they cry. "Hey, I'm really not that bad." They do whatever it takes to get back to that comfort zone between success and failure. Most significantly, whether winning or losing, they forfeit the opportunity to learn from their experiences. They won't risk failure, and because of this, they never grow as winners.

REVERSING THE IMAGE

It's a paradox that so many companies, while investing in state-of-the-art business technology, remain in the Dark Ages when it comes to incorporating modern behavioral knowledge into their sales training structure. They're big on drilling their salespeople on technique, but at the same time, they neglect to address their workers' negative self-images. Make no mistake; at-leasters are smart and skilled. They learn new techniques quickly enough, but their lack of internal reprogramming negates all this packaging. The result: more seesaw sales performance, more new salespeople to add to the staff, more training programs, more money spent, and fewer positive results.

Without the proper inner resources, even the best skills in the world won't make a sale, and all this fine-tuning simply shackles the organization with a disproportionate share of unhappy at-leasters. Given the fact that at-leasters are a common product of the way we're brought up, how can a sales organization convert them into winners?

A profile of winners shows that these people have internal resources that outside negativity just won't erode. Here are a few examples:

✗ Winners are self-motivated; they believe in themselves and feel they make a difference. They're driven by a "fire in the belly" and won't be corrupted by naysayers. They've got their priorities straight. Winners have the tools that keep their internal belief systems running, repairing, and revitalizing themselves every day, every hour.

✗ When winners don't feel good, they act as if they do. This isn't brainwashing or denial; it's purely a technique for getting over the hump until that original spontaneity comes back.

✗ Winners prepare for a challenge by thinking positively. They focus on instances in their lives where they truly wanted something and got it.

✗ Winners literally keep their heads up. They keep smiling no matter how hard their opponent is trying to beat them down. Just try to feel lousy while looking up at the sky. Tough, isn't it?

✗ Winners build a support group of positive people around them, even though their background, circumstances, or social circle may not have given them that support when they were growing up. Winners know they can't change the past, but they can create a healthy environment in the present—which carries them into the future with optimism and positive feelings.

Last and Definitely Least . . .

Bronze Clients: The low 20 percent, bronze clients may bring in 5 percent of your business—and that's a good bronze client! Your bad bronze clients bring in around 1 percent of your business and provide more opportunities for wasted effort than all your other clients combined.

One type of bronze client wants more service for less money. They'll hang around for many years, demand 80 percent of your time, and deliver almost no business. My recommendation? *Get rid of them*—as soon as possible—making more room for gold and platinum clients. The second type of bronze client is the brand new client who's just signed up. It's your job to nurture and grow them into silver, gold, and platinum clients—or give them to someone who needs the business.

In fact, when you bring in clients, ask yourself how much you like them as people, not just for the business or buying and selling. If you don't like most of your clients, if they are not respectful of your values, think hard about what and to whom you are selling.

The Bottom Line

The bottom line is *you*, regardless of the product or service. How good a resource person are you? If you work for a company that isn't providing you with the training, resources, or quality product to make you a significant resource for your clients, then you have to find ways to make a difference. Those days when you kept one job for twenty years and were perceived as loyal and hard working are gone. Today, if you are with one company for twenty years, people think something may be wrong with you.

Keeping Track

Organizing your clients into either platinum-, gold-, silver-, and bronze-level categories enables you to use your time in more productive ways. Here then are some ready-made forms for doing just that. Use them to organize your client list in a way that will be much more meaningful and useful to you, and to keep detailed records of your activities in keeping them happy or moving them up the scale.

PLATINUM CLIENTS
(4 percent—to be contacted monthly)

Client 1

Name: _____

Company: _____

Product/Service: _____

Why Platinum? _____

Phone: _____

Service Activity Record: _____

_____

_____

_____

Client 2

Name: _____

Company: _____

Product/Service: _____

Why Platinum? _____

Phone: _____

Service Activity Record: _____

_____

_____

_____

Client 3

Name: _____

Company: _____

Product/Service: _____

Why Platinum?_____

Phone:_____

Service Activity Record:_____

_____

_____

_____

Client 4

Name:_____

Company:_____

Product/Service:_____

Why Platinum?_____

Phone:_____

Service Activity Record:_____

_____

_____

_____

Client 5

Name:_____

Company:_____

Product/Service:_____

Why Platinum?_____

Phone:_____

Service Activity Record:_____

_____

_____

_____

GOLD CLIENTS
(20 percent—includes Platinums—to be contacted monthly)

Client 1

Name: _____

Company: _____

Product/Service: _____

Why Gold? _____

Phone: _____

Service Activity Record: _____

_____

_____

_____

Client 2

Name: _____

Company: _____

Product/Service: _____

Why Gold? _____

Phone: _____

Service Activity Record: _____

_____

_____

_____

Client 3

Name: _____

Company: _____

Product/Service: _____

Why Gold?_____

Phone:_____

Service Activity Record:_____

_____

_____

_____

Client 4

Name:_____

Company:_____

Product/Service:_____

Why Gold?_____

Phone:_____

Service Activity Record:_____

_____

_____

_____

Client 5

Name:_____

Company:_____

Product/Service:_____

Why Gold?_____

Phone:_____

Service Activity Record:_____

_____

_____

_____

SILVER CLIENTS
(60 percent — to be contacted quarterly)

Client 1

Name: _____

Company: _____

Product/Service: _____

Why Silver? _____

Phone: _____

Service Activity Record: _____

_____

_____

_____

Client 2

Name: _____

Company: _____

Product/Service: _____

Why Silver? _____

Phone: _____

Service Activity Record: _____

_____

_____

_____

Client 3

Name: _____

Company: _____

Product/Service: _____

Why Silver? _____

Phone: _____

Service Activity Record: _____

_____

_____

_____

Client 4

Name: _____

Company: _____

Product/Service: _____

Why Silver? _____

Phone: _____

Service Activity Record: _____

_____

_____

_____

Client 5

Name: _____

Company: _____

Product/Service: _____

Why Silver? _____

Phone: _____

Service Activity Record: _____

_____

_____

_____

BRONZE CLIENTS
(20 percent—to be contacted every six months, upgraded, or eliminated)

Client 1

Name: _____

Company: _____

Product/Service: _____

Why Bronze? _____

Phone: _____

Service Activity Record: _____

_____

_____

_____

Client 2

Name: _____

Company: _____

Product/Service: _____

Why Bronze? _____

Phone: _____

Service Activity Record: _____

_____

_____

_____

Client 3

Name: _____

Company: _____

Product/Service: _____

Why Bronze? _____

Phone: _____

Service Activity Record: _____

_____

_____

_____

Client 4

Name: _____

Company: _____

Product/Service: _____

Why Bronze? _____

Phone: _____

Service Activity Record: _____

_____

_____

_____

Client 5

Name: _____

Company: _____

Product/Service: _____

Why Bronze? _____

Phone: _____

Service Activity Record: _____

_____

_____

_____

Chapter 17 Summary

1. *Platinum Clients:* The top 4 percent of the people you do business with. They come from the gold clients. They are unconditional givers. Take very good care of them and let them take care of you too. If you don't ask for help, a referral, advice, counsel, information, they may stay a client, but if a stranger asks for help, they'll give that info to them.

2. *Gold Clients:* The top 20 percent—they bring in 80 percent of the revenues, referrals, and introductions. Stay in contact on a regular basis, quarterly at least. Build relationships with them to get and sell and to be a resource person for them.

3. *Silver Clients:* 60 percent of the typical client base, they bring in 15 percent of your business.

4. *Bronze Clients:* 20 percent, but they bring in 5 percent of your business at most, usually less. These either have been around for a while, are not your favorites, and want more service for less money, or they are brand new, just having signed up. It's your job to eliminate the old ones and winnow out and try to build and grow the new ones into silver, gold, and platinum clients—or give them to someone who needs the business.

Because of the intensity of competition, in order to keep clients, you must set up gold and silvers and know who the platinums are, and I strongly suggest you get rid of the negative bronzes. To grow your business, you will have to drop off 5–10 percent of the bottom.

When you bring in clients, ask yourself how much you like them as people, not just for their business or buying and selling. If you don't like most of your clients, if they are not respectful of your values, think hard about what you are selling and to whom you are selling.

marketing strategies for selling professionals

THERE ARE NUMEROUS ways to attract new prospects and clients to you and your business, some of which can be done at low or even no cost. In this chapter, I'll assume that you have the appropriate brochure, business card, Web site—or at least a Web page—and a simple press kit with your photo, bio, and a list of what you and/or your products and services can do to make a difference.

If not, then you may not be ready to take advantage of many of these tips. In that case, you need to do some work to prepare yourself. On the other hand, if you're ready, here's a list of the most *positive* and *powerful* ways to attract those individuals and organizations with whom you'd like to build relationships and do business.

Twenty-Five Low Cost Ways to Attract New Prospects and Clients Without Having to Cold Call

25. PRINT AND RADIO ADVERTISING

This method is probably the most expensive and least effective,

202 YOUR SUCCESSFUL SALES CAREER

because you definitely have to continue to advertise yourself, your product, or services consistently (at least five or six times) to determine the effectiveness and overall success of the ad. You need the time and repetition to test and adjust the script.

While radio advertising can be surprisingly affordable, I would suggest that you retain a media professional, such as a copywriter or media marketing person, so that you can get the best advice and counsel, along with copy that works well for you.

24. DIRECTORY LISTINGS

There are two types of directory listings available. One may be free or low cost. The other can be quite expensive. Also, since listings are "passive" advertising and there's no guarantee of success, results may be poor. The exception might be your local chamber of commerce or specialty association trade directory.

Free or low cost listings may be available in special directories, which can be listed in a Directory of Directories found in major business libraries. You need to do some research to find, contact, and get listed in the right ones.

23. RADIO, TELEVISION, CABLE, AND PRINT INTERVIEWS

Almost any library with a good business shelf has public relations directories, such as Burrelle's or Bacon's, which list those shows that use interviews as well as, in many cases, the people who book guests. An alternative approach is to check your local TV listings, identify those shows that you would like to contact, call or e-mail the producer directly, and "pitch them" on your "unique" idea or slant. This is number 23 because you need good luck, timing, and/ or something hot to present before getting your shot. This same approach can work for your local newspaper or a very good PR/marketing company.

22. MASS MAILINGS

Many large companies still do mass mailings to both suspects and prospects. In the past (five years or more ago), this may have been successful and produced results (about 1 percent response for the first round of mailings). These days, companies use mass mailings for "presence" or in collaboration with other related vendors. There are still a few mass mail vendors, such as Val-Pak, that package your message, along with others, and do a mass mailing in a designated area or zip code.

Some marketing companies promote a mailing using targeted lists. This could be the effective response called for in the mailing piece. Make sure you *always* have your Web site and/or e-mail address included on the mailer.

21. PERSONALIZED DIRECT MAIL

Here, your computer is harnessed to produce targeted letters to qualified prospects. Their names may be found in newspapers, magazines, or trade publications. A well-written, personal letter can still be an effective way to attract business and attention to your company.

Here are some helpful tips when utilizing the direct mail approach:

Always combine a direct mail program with telephone and e-mail follow-up.

Always send the letter to a specific C-level executive, i.e., a decision maker (CEO, COO, CIO, CFO, or VP of sales, marketing, or HR), rather than to just a functional title.

Always use typed or handwritten letterhead stationary and envelopes.

Do not send form letters!

Always tailor your letter to the "wants, needs, or concerns" of your "suspects," market, or industry. Make sure you include a "unique value proposition" in order to capture their attention quickly, so that they are favorably predisposed to your message.

20. SPECIAL PROMOTIONS, DONATIONS, PREMIUMS, AND INCENTIVES

You can enhance your image and gain valuable exposure through joint promotion with other organizations by cosponsoring a fundraiser or business event or even volunteering your time to a charity or nonprofit function. Give away a useful and tasteful premium or incentive at a tradeshow or as a special token to remind clients and prospects of your presence and availability.

19. TRADE SHOWS, CONFERENCES, AND EXPOSITIONS

There are two strategies: (1) when you exhibit and (2) when you attend.

1. Almost 80 percent of all exhibitors commit at least two common mistakes at trade shows, conferences, and business expositions:

   a. Not asking the right questions to identify a qualified prospect

   b. Not following up *all* inquiries in a timely and meaningful way

2. As a visitor, you can connect with *both* attendees *and* exhibitors and qualify them by finding out about their products and services, as well as their needs, as they relate to your product or service, so that you can follow them up.

18. PROFESSIONAL AND TRADE ASSOCIATIONS AND MEETINGS

With the proliferation of business, professional, and trade associations available, you need to do some research and fieldwork to discover which organizations are right for you, both economically and socially, and in that order. Once you have identified the two or three right ones (you can join more if you have deep pockets and plenty of time), you must then visit them once or twice as a guest to observe and then interview the key players of the organization. When you've joined, be prepared to become actively involved with at least one committee in each organization. Solid relationships start and get built at these levels and above.

17. SEMINARS AND WORKSHOPS

There are two strategies here: (1) when you give one, and (2) when you take one.

1. *Giving a seminar or workshop.* You can either put on your own or seek out those organizations and associations . . . *including your own* . . . that already sponsor seminars and workshops.

   Your local chamber of commerce is an excellent resource, along with local community colleges. Making a presentation or putting on a workshop defines you as an expert in your field.

2. *Taking a seminar or workshop.* This is a great way to gain knowledge and information about what is currently going on in your market or industry, as well as add to your toolbox of skills and resources.

   If you also register and take some workshops that your ideal prospect may take, your presence allows you to connect and network with those prospects in a safe, nonselling environment.

16. WRITING MAGAZINE AND TRADE ARTICLES

First, do some research in your market and industry and find out what's hot and what's not. If you can't, don't like to, or don't want to write the article, you can find many freelance writers in your community who will. Check your local IABC chapter (International Association of Business Communicators) and contact it for writers. You can also go to your local college, visit the journalism or communications departments, and ask for help. Never hype yourself or your company in the article, but do have a one-sentence description of yourself with contact information at the conclusion of the article, along with a photo, if possible.

15. PUBLIC SPEECHES AND LECTURES

Whether it's local civic groups, such as the Rotary, Lions, Jaycees, or 4H, or business groups like the chamber of commerce or adult education at a local community college, most organizations like to have outside speakers at their meetings. Contact the program chairperson to discuss the possibility of speaking to their group. (Note: Many groups might even pay you. At the very least, they'll probably feed you.) If you're not sure you're a good speaker yet or want to be better, contact your local Toastmasters chapter and attend some meetings. It's also a great place to network.

14. BUSINESS CARDS

Your business card is your "calling card!" Make sure it looks professional and has some identifiable information about who you are and what you do. Before you decide to print your cards, do some research of your own. Select two or three cards that you find appealing and attractive from those business cards that you've received over the past year or two. Check out the cards your major competitors are giving out and see what you do or do not like and what you might learn from. Remember: Your business card is another form of advertising, albeit, a passive type.

13. BROCHURE

Simple, attractive, and to the point, a brochure that is read is worth more to your sales strategy than one that is put in the "file it" pile. Two colors are more effective than one, but four colors are superfluous. There are exceptions, of course. Action photographs and strong graphics can add dimension; just be sure you use good quality paper. As with business cards (see no. 14), check out what your major competitor uses and see what you like and don't like. Learning from others' successes and failures can save you a lot of time and money!

12. AUDIO, VIDEO, OR CD BUSINESS CARDS

Within the past six years, the creation and use of audio, video, and even CD business cards has been added to some companies' advertising and marketing budgets. The purpose is to use them for direct mail and prospecting, along with having them as handouts at trade shows, expositions, and conferences. If you have the budget and a PR or marketing professional with the appropriate expertise to create a slick, attractive piece, then do it. Be sure you select and carefully target your intended market and follow up immediately, with a subtle request to forward it on to an appropriate person, if they have no need or interest.

11. AUDIT BUSINESS CARDS

While giving out 3,000 business cards or more each year may make you think you are going to get a lot of business (your printer is really the one getting the business), the number of cards you *collect and take action on* really help you get more business. When you ask for or receive someone's business card, check the information, turn the card around, and write something on the back of it that might be important, for example, the date, place, and a time to call back or follow up. Let the person know you're making a note.

It might be to just follow up or send something you think might be of value. Then make sure you do it quickly and elegantly.

The Top Ten Ways to Attract Business Without Cold Calling

10. LEADERSHIP IN THE COMMUNITY

This critical but subtle strategy cannot be rushed. Find a charity or nonprofit organization that you feel passionate about or would like to help make a difference. You must first have a sincere desire for the organization and/or their cause to which you would like to commit some time and energy. You may not realize it, but you could be working shoulder-to-shoulder with others who may be influential in referring you to their or other organizations that might benefit from your talent, skills, or abilities, if not your products or services. Just remember: It first takes time, patience, and commitment on your part.

9. PUBLISHING YOUR OWN NEWSLETTER

If you're first starting out, you may only have the time and patience to publish and distribute your newsletter quarterly (spring, summer, fall, winter). If you want credibility and long-standing presence, you must have something that is regularly updated and informational. There are professional and freelance writers who can write the content, if necessary. Also, there are companies who have standard "niche" newsletters available. All you do is provide your company logo, address, contact information, and photo for insertion. They will produce and, sometimes, even distribute your newsletter. Eventually, you'll want to publish a monthly or bimonthly newsletter. You might even do it via e-mail (see no. 1, The Internet and Your Web Site).

8. COLLEAGUES, PEERS, AND ASSOCIATES

Some of these people may be those whom you knew in your previous job or industry association. They thought well of you then, but somehow they've lost track of you along the way. You can rekindle those connections once again and track where they lead. In addition, be aware of others that you know in a related field or industry, whose introductions and referrals could be of value to you. One of the easiest and best ways to keep in "quality contact" with these people is through your newsletter (see no. 9, Publishing Your Own Newsletter).

7. BUILDING YOUR OWN "HOUSE LIST"

This is imperative to your success and growth. Invest in a good database software program or retain a quality professional vendor to keep and maintain one for you. I use www.Webvalence.com, for my e-mail newsletter and database management. Your list will produce, on average, five to ten times the response of any outside list you buy or rent. The names can come from clients, colleagues, associates, business cards you collect, membership lists of associations in which you participate, or your own address book. Make sure you keep this list updated and current.

6. LETTERS OF INTRODUCTION, ENDORSEMENTS, AND REFERRALS

A very powerful, credible way of attracting new business is through letters of introduction. In Asia and the Middle East especially, letters of introduction from satisfied clients to one of their colleagues, associates, or clients carries a great deal of weight. It opens many doors, which may not ordinarily be accessed. You can ask your "gold" clients (your top 20 percent) to write an "endorsement" describing your skill, ability, and what you've been able to accomplish for them or help them achieve. Then ask them if you can mail it to their colleagues, associates, and/or clients as well.

5. AZAR'S 80/20/20 THEORY

Typically, you will find that 80 percent of your business, quality introductions, and referrals come from about 20 percent of your clients (gold). Your gold clients are sold on you and your business. Furthermore, 20 percent of your gold clients are willing—*if you ask them*—to work for you in offering leads and recommending new clients for your business. Treat them with care and attention and they will be instrumental in helping you grow your business. You must acknowledge and recognize them on a regular basis. In some circles, they are also known as "golden geese." Don't kill them to get their eggs!

4. FORMAL AND INFORMAL NETWORKING

There are many opportunities to "press the flesh" in the business world. For you to be successful in attracting new business, you must be socially attuned and be able to rub elbows with those you wish to do business with or who have access to those you wish to meet. If you are not amenable to doing this, for your sake, have someone in your organization who is and wants to be active in this role. Then let them plant seeds.

There are many places to network: chamber of commerce "after hours" events, conferences, trade shows, seminars, workshops, and Toastmasters. Every major city has a number of "formal networks," that is, networks formed to do business within its membership. Some organized groups that may be listed are BNI, Le Tips, and Power Core. Many local chambers of commerce have their own "leads" groups, as well.

3. POWER NETWORKS

A successful power network can represent the difference between the professional and the amateur when it comes to building relationships and doing business. A strong, healthy, power network is a safe environment to share ideas, information, and resources. The members of a power network must be in separate, noncompetitive companies or markets. Their products or services can be related or supplemental in nature. Each member is a resource person who knows how to connect people as well as be connected. Some of the members may even qualify to be included in your "MasterMind" (see no. 2, Creating a MasterMind, for an explanation).

2. CREATING A MASTERMIND

A MasterMind is a group of like-minded, positive, supportive individuals who are in similar or related industries or professions. They are committed to meeting on a regular basis and assisting each other in various ways. The members come from several places, including chambers of commerce, associations, and power networks. They can be made up of mentors, friends, colleagues, clients, vendors, etc. They may be accountants, lawyers, PR professionals, entrepreneurs, corporate executives, real estate professionals, bankers, brokers, insurance specialists, business coaches, health or wellness specialists, spiritual advisers, doctors, or educators, each with their unique blend of talent, skills, and abilities. It may take up to a year to form your MasterMind fully, but it will be well worth the time, patience, and energy you put into this creation.

1. THE INTERNET AND YOUR WEB SITE

With a multitude of capabilities and unlimited opportunities, the Internet is rapidly changing the way we do business. Without your own Web site, even if you use it only for e-mail, presence, and contact information, you are far behind the curve of success. By having your own Web site and using the Internet for marketing, advertising, or, at the very least, prospecting for new business, you are truly stepping up in productivity. By creating an attractive, user-friendly Web site, even the smallest entrepreneur can be on a similar playing field to big business.

Utilizing the power of the Internet can help you build the perception of a global business. As it evolves with newer technology, including better audio and video capabilities, you may apply those tools to your Web site and create new and different ways to enhance your business, its products, and services. If you want to be a savvy businessperson, you have to harness its capabilities, its creativity and productivity benefits. Make the investment of time, energy, and money to educate yourself on this exciting breakthrough technology. If you're not technical, like me, you want to find the best and brightest Internet and Web specialists available and add them to your team, perhaps even your MasterMind.

Chapter 18 Summary

Utilize as many of the Twenty-Five Ways to Attract Clients list as fit your or your company's marketing model to build your sales as well as your reputation as a sales professional.

Recommended Resources

MAGAZINES

Selling Power

Sales and Marketing Management

Inc.

Entrepreneur

Fast Company

BOOKS

Berman Fortgang, Laura. *Take Yourself to the Top: The Secrets of America's #1 Career Coach*. New York: Warner Books, 1998.

Boress, Allan. *The "I Hate Selling" Book*. New York: Amacom, 1995.

Canfield, Jack, and Mark Victor Hansen. *The Aladdin Factor*. Berkley Books, 1995.

Collins, Jim. *Good to Great: Why Some Companies Make the Leap—and Others Don't*. New York: HarperBusiness, 2001.

Covey, Stephen. *The Seven Habits of Highly Effective People: Restoring the Character Ethic*. Thorndike, ME: G. K. Hall, 1997.

Gallagher, William. *Guerrilla Selling*. Boston: Houghton Mifflin, 1992.

Gerber, Michael. *The E Myth: Why Most Contractors' Businesses Don't Work and What to Do About It*. New York: HarperBusiness, 2002.

Hall, Doug. *Jump Start Your Business Brain: Win More, Lose Less and Make More Money with Your New Products, Services, Sales and Advertising*. Cincinnati: Brain Brew Books, 2001.

Hill, Napoleon. *Think and Grow Rich*. Encino, CA: Briggs Publishing, 2003.

Loehr, James E. *Toughness Training for Life: A Revolutionary Program for Maximizing Health, Happiness, and Productivity*. New York: Dutton, 1993.

Ries, Al, and Laura Ries. *The Fall of Advertising and the Rise of PR*. New York: HarperBusiness, 2002.

Robbins, Anthony. *Unlimited Power*. New York: Simon & Schuster, 1997.

Sanders, Tim. *Love Is the Killer APP: How to Win Business and Influence Friends*. New York: Crown Business, 2002.

Weiss, Alan. *Million Dollar Consulting: The Professional's Guide to Growing a Practice*. New York: McGraw-Hill, 2003.

ONLINE SALES TRAINING

www.salesdoctor.com

www.nosuckersales.com

www.ihateselling.com

INSPIRATIONAL VIDEOS

Rocky (1976), *Spartacus* (1960), *The Star Wars Trilogy: Star Wars* (1977), *The Empire Strikes Back* (1980), *Return of the Jedi* (1983), *A Christmas Carol* (1951, 1984), *One Flew Over the Cuckoo's Nest* (1975), *The Good, the Bad, and the Ugly* (1966), *On the Waterfront* (1954),

Rudy (1993), *Cool Hand Luke* (1967), *Fearless* (1993), *The Shawshank Redemption* (1994), *Braveheart* (1995), *Cast Away* (2000), *The Great Escape* (1963), *Glengarry Glen Ross* (1992), *The Boiler Room* (2000), *Seasbiscuit* (2003).

USEFUL WEB SITES
Web Site Development and Hosting
www.webvalence.com

www.crosscomm.com

www.mazu.com

www.trianglewebnet.com

Personal, Professional, Executive, or Sales Coaching
www.CoachingCatalyst.com

www.SalesDoctor.com

Financial Coaching
www.moneyful.com, ask for Genevia

Voice, Diction, or Voiceover Coaching
www.voiceoversUnlimited.com, ask for Dan

Online Copywriting
www.ultimatewealth.com

www.surefiremarketing.com

www.makeitwrite.com

Online Sales and Marketing Tools
www.ecovergenerator.com

www.headergenerator.com

www.linkcheckgenerator.com

TRAINING AND PRACTICE IN SPEAKING

Toastmasters International

National Speakers Association

American Society for Training and Development (ASTD)

Index